CONTENTS

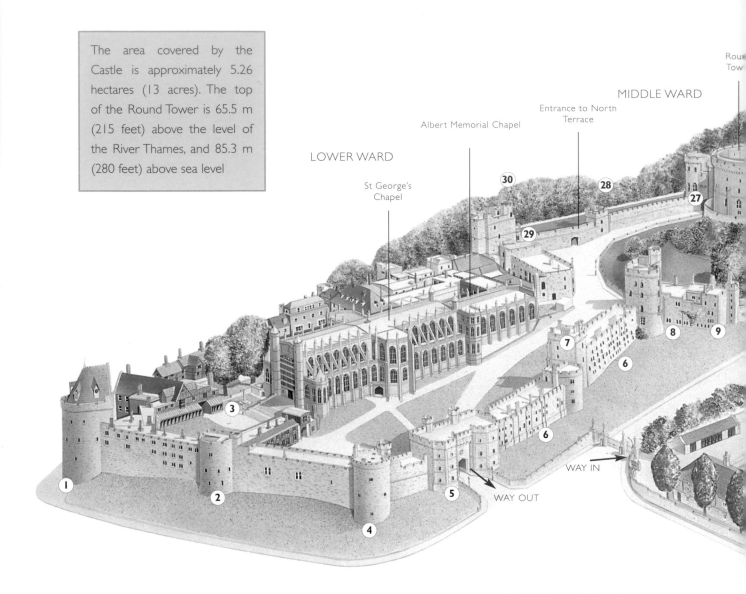

The area covered by the Castle is approximately 5.26 hectares (13 acres). The top of the Round Tower is 65.5 m (215 feet) above the level of the River Thames, and 85.3 m (280 feet) above sea level

MIDDLE WARD

Entrance to North Terrace

Albert Memorial Chapel

LOWER WARD

St George's Chapel

WAY IN

WAY OUT

KEY		
1 Curfew Tower	**14** York Tower	**17** Clarence Tower
2 Garter Tower	**15** Augusta Tower	**18** Chester Tower
3 Horseshoe Cloister	**16** Queen's Tower	**19** Prince of Wales's Tower
4 Salisbury Tower		**20** Brunswick Tower
5 King Henry VIII Gate		**21** State Entrance
6 Military Knights' Lodgings		**22** The Quadrangle
7 Mary Tudor Tower		**23** King George IV Tower
8 King Henry III Tower		**24** King John's Tower
9 Saxon Tower		**25** King Charles II Statue
10 St George's Gate		**26** Engine Court
11 King Edward III Tower		**27** Norman Gate
12 Lancaster Tower		**28** Magazine Tower
13 King George IV Gate		**29** Store Tower
		30 Winchester Tower

State Apartments,
The Gallery and
en Mary's Dolls' House

UPPER WARD

North Terrace (east end)
open August and September only

astle Hill

Castle Education
Centre

THE DEVELOPMENT OF THE CASTLE

The existing vast structure has evolved over many centuries from its origin as a Norman fortress. Windsor Castle is the oldest royal residence to have remained in continuous use by the monarchs of Britain and is in many ways an architectural epitome of the history of the nation. The Castle covers an area of about 5 hectares (13 acres) and contains, as well as a royal palace, a magnificent collegiate church and the homes or workplaces of a large number of people, including the Constable and Governor of the Castle, the Military Knights of Windsor and the Dean and Canons of St George's Chapel.

The earliest part of the structure is the artificial earthen mound in the middle which was raised *c.*1080 by William the Conqueror. It supports the Round Tower built by Henry II, who adapted a purely defensive fortification as a residence by building the first royal apartments on the north side of the Upper Ward. The Upper Ward was converted into a huge Gothic palace by a succession of medieval kings, notably Edward III in the fourteenth century. He also founded the Order of the Garter and the associated College of St George in the Lower Ward. Edward IV built the present St George's Chapel in the fifteenth century. Charles II reconstructed the State Apartments in Baroque taste in the 1670s, and the whole of the Upper Ward was reconstructed to its present picturesque Gothic appearance and the Round Tower heightened by George IV in the 1820s. He was also responsible for acquiring much of the magnificent art collection which now fills the rooms of the Castle. Following a serious fire in 1992, a new roof was designed for St George's Hall, and the adjoining Lantern Lobby and the Private Chapel were rebuilt in modern Gothic style.

HISTORY OF THE CASTLE

ORIGINS

The Castle was founded by William the Conqueror *c.*1080 as one of a chain of fortifications round London. It occupies the only naturally defensive site in this part of the Thames Valley, 30 metres (100 feet) above the river.

Norman castles were built to a standard plan with an artificial mound (motte) supporting a keep, the entrance to which was protected by a fenced yard or bailey. Windsor is the most notable example of a distinctive version of this plan developed for use on a ridge, with baileys on both sides of a central motte.

When first built, the Castle was entirely defensive, but easy access from London and proximity to the old royal hunting forest (now Windsor Great Park) soon recommended it as a royal residence. Henry I had domestic quarters within the Castle as early as 1110 and Henry II built two separate sets of apartments, a state residence in the Lower Ward, with a hall where he could entertain his court on great occasions, and a smaller residence on the north side of the Upper Ward for his family's exclusive occupation.

Henry II also began to replace the timber outer walls of the Upper Ward in stone. The basic curtain wall, modified by later alterations, dates from Henry II's time, as does the Round Tower on top of the motte. The curtain wall round the Lower Ward was completed over the next sixty years. The well-preserved section visible from the High Street with three half-round towers was built by Henry III in the 1220s. He carried out extensive works at Windsor, rebuilding Henry II's apartments in the Lower Ward and adding a new Chapel; parts survive embedded in later structures in the Lower Ward. He also further improved the royal apartments in the Upper Ward.

William I (b.1027) 1066–1087

1080
Construction in earth and timber begins; present plan established

Henry II (b.1133) 1154–1189

1170s
Castle largely rebuilt in stone, with square towers in curtain wall, and Round Tower on motte

Henry III (b.1207) 1216–1272

1220s
West wall rebuilt in stone and five rounded towers added to curtain wall.

1240–1248
Royal Chapel constructed on site of present Albert Memorial Chapel in Lower Ward

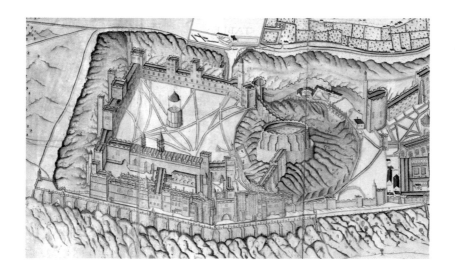

MEDIEVAL RECONSTRUCTION

The outstanding medieval expansion of Windsor took place in the reign of Edward III (1327–77). The Castle was converted into a Gothic palace and the seat of the new Order of the Garter. The massive architecture of Windsor reflects Edward III's medieval ideal of Christian, chivalric monarchy as clearly as Louis XIV's Versailles represents seventeenth-century centralisation and Divine Right.

The Lower Ward was transformed for the College of St George. Founded on 6 August 1348, the College comprised the Dean, twelve Canons, and thirteen Vicars-Choral to conduct regular services. In addition there were to be twenty-six Poor Knights to represent the Knights of the Garter at daily services.

The reconstruction of the Upper Ward began in 1357 under the direction of William of Wykeham, Bishop of Winchester. An inner gatehouse with cylindrical towers (now misleadingly called the 'Norman Gate') was built. Stone-vaulted undercrofts (which survive) supported extensive royal apartments on the first floor with separate rooms for the King and Queen (in the tradition of English royal palaces), arranged round inner courtyards. Along the south side, facing the quadrangle, were the Great Hall and Royal Chapel end to end.

Edward III (b. 1312) 1327–1377

1358–1368
Upper Ward reconstructed as large royal palace with new St George's Hall and 'Norman Gate'

Edward IV (b.1442) 1461–1483

1475–1483
St George's Chapel and new Cloisters built

Henry VIII (b. 1491) 1509–1547

1511
New gate to Lower Ward built

Mary I (b.1516) 1553–1558

1550
Military Knights' Houses in Lower Ward constructed

ABOVE: *Bird's Eye View of Windsor Castle,* by Wenceslaus Hollar, 1672

Edward III's State Apartments survived down to the seventeenth century, the later medieval kings hardly altering them. Edward IV built the present St George's Chapel to the west of Henry III's Chapel. Henry VII remodelled the old Chapel (now the Albert Memorial Chapel) at its east end; he also added a new range to the west of the State Apartments which Elizabeth I extended by a Long Gallery (all now occupied by the Royal Library). Henry VIII built the entrance gateway to the Lower Ward, and his daughter, Queen Mary, built the lodgings for the Military Knights on the south side of the Lower Ward.

CHARLES II'S BAROQUE PALACE

During the English Civil War in the mid-seventeenth century, the Castle was seized by Parliamentary forces who used it as a prison. King Charles I was buried in St George's Chapel after his execution at Whitehall in 1649.

On the Restoration of the monarchy in 1660 Charles II determined to reinstate Windsor as his principal non-metropolitan palace. The architect Hugh May was appointed in 1673 to supervise the work, which took eleven years to complete. May kept the blocky, castellated exterior but regularised the elevations and inserted round-arched windows, some of which are still visible today.

The interior was a rich contrast and contained the grandest Baroque State Apartments in England. The arrangement of duplicated sets for the King and Queen was kept but expanded. The walls were wainscoted in oak and festooned with brilliant virtuoso carvings

Elizabeth I (b. 1533) 1558–1603

1580
Long Gallery added to State Apartments (now Royal Library)

Charles I (b. 1600) 1625–1649

m. Henrietta Maria (b. 1609, d. 1669)

1649
Charles I buried at Windsor after execution at Whitehall

Interregnum 1649–1660

Interregnum (Oliver Cromwell, Lord Protector)

by Grinling Gibbons and Henry Phillips. The ceilings were painted by Antonio Verrio, an Italian artist brought to Windsor from Paris by the Duke of Montagu. Only those in the Queen's Presence and Audience Chambers and the King's Dining Room have survived, but the general form and proportions of the State Apartments are as created by Charles II.

ABOVE: *The North Terrace Looking West*, by Paul Sandby, c. 1780

PICTURESQUE REVIVAL

William III and the early Hanoverian kings preferred Hampton Court to Windsor; however, George III chose it as his favourite residence. After recovery from his first illness in 1789, the King decided to move into the Castle. He initiated extensive works to the design of James Wyatt, who began to convert Hugh May's windows to Gothic and to lighten the appearance of the state rooms by replacing the wainscot with coloured damasks. At the same time a new state entrance and Gothic staircase were constructed. The State Apartments of the Upper Ward and precincts were open to the public on a regular basis by George III's reign.

When George IV inherited the throne in 1820, he determined to continue the Gothic transformation of the exterior and the creation of comfortable and splendid new royal apartments. In his proposals for Windsor, George IV was influenced by his chief artistic adviser, Sir Charles Long. It was decided in 1823 to hold a limited competition for the work and Long drew up an informal brief. Its principal points were the heightening of Henry II's Round Tower,

Charles II (b. 1630) 1660–1685

m. **Catherine (b. 1638, d. 1705)**

1660
Restoration of monarchy

1673–1684
State Apartments in Upper Ward remodelled as Baroque palace. Long Walk laid out

George III (b. 1738) 1760–1820

m. **Charlotte (b. 1744, d. 1818)**

1789–1806
Gothic reconstruction of State Apartments begun. Frogmore acquired and Parks improved

ABOVE: The East Front

the general enhancement of the silhouette with extra towers and battlements, the addition of the Grand Corridor round the Upper Ward, the creation of the Waterloo Chamber to celebrate the Allied victory over Napoleon, the continuation up to the Castle of the Long Walk instituted by Charles II, and the making of the King George IV Gateway. Three leading architects, Sir John Soane, Sir Robert Smirke and John Nash, were asked to submit plans, as was the late James Wyatt's nephew Jeffry. The job was given to the last named. He carried out Long's programme to the last detail, creating the present appearance of the Upper Ward, earning a knighthood and medievalising his surname to Wyatville. Inside the Castle new private rooms were made as a setting for George IV's rich collections, and the old Hall and Chapel were knocked together to create a vast Gothic-revival St George's Hall. Charles II's state rooms were refurbished, this work continuing (still under Wyatville's direction) into the reign of William IV. George IV himself took up residence in the Castle in 1828.

QUEEN VICTORIA AND THE TWENTIETH CENTURY

In many ways Windsor Castle reached its apogee in the reign of Queen Victoria. She spent the greatest portion of every year at Windsor, and in her reign it enjoyed the position of principal palace of the British monarchy and the focus of the British Empire as well

George IV (b. 1762) 1820–1830

m. Caroline (b. 1768, d. 1821)

1823–1830
Completion of Gothic reconstruction.
Round Tower heightened. Grand
Corridor added. New royal apartments
and State Apartments remodelled

Queen Victoria (b. 1819) 1837–1901

m. Albert (b. 1819, d. 1861)

1861
Her husband Prince Albert dies at Windsor

1861–1866
Lower Ward restored. Grand Staircase to
State Apartments rebuilt

LEFT: *Sunday Morning in the Lower Ward*, by Joseph Nash, 1846

BELOW: Photograph of Her Majesty The Queen in Garter Robes by Sir Cecil Beaton, 1956

as nearly the whole of royal Europe (many members of which were the Queen's relations). The Castle was visited by Heads of State from all over the world. On these occasions the state rooms were used for their original purpose by royal guests.

Wyatville and George IV had left the Castle in such splendid order that no major work was required. Queen Victoria made a few minor alterations, reconstructing the Grand Staircase and contriving a new Private Chapel (burnt in 1992) to the design of Edward Blore. In the Lower Ward the Curfew Tower and Horseshoe Cloisters were both restored, and the disused Chapel east of St George's was remodelled with marble and mosaic as a memorial to Prince Albert, who died at Windsor Castle on 14 December 1861.

For most of the twentieth century the Castle survived as it was in the nineteenth century.

George V (b. 1865) 1910–1936

m. **Mary (b. 1867, d. 1953)**

**1911–1914
State Apartments refurbished**

George VI (b. 1895) 1936–1952

m. **Elizabeth (b. 1900)**

**1947
Garter Procession and Service in
St George's Chapel revived**

**1952
Buried at Windsor**

Elizabeth II (b. 1926) 1952–

m. **Philip (b. 1921)**

**1992–1997
Castle restored after serious
fire damage**

THE FIRE OF 1992

On 20 November 1992 a serious fire broke out in the Private Chapel at the north-east angle of the Upper Ward. It is thought to have been caused by a spotlight igniting a curtain high up over the altar. Despite the efforts of the Castle staff and the fire brigade, the fire spread rapidly at roof level, destroying the ceilings of George IV's St George's Hall and Grand Reception Room as well as gutting the Private Chapel, the State Dining Room, the Crimson Drawing Room and various subsidiary rooms. By great good fortune the rooms worst affected by the fire were empty at the time as they were in the course of being rewired. As a result few of the Castle's artistic treasures were destroyed. The principal casualties were a fitted sideboard and a painting, *George III at a Review* by Sir William Beechey, both of which were too big to move.

ABOVE: The fire in the Upper Ward, 1992

BELOW: A craftsmen at work restoring the fire-damaged Grand Reception Room

ABOVE: Her Majesty The Queen inspecting the damage in St George's Hall after the fire of November 1992

RESTORATION

The work of repair began immediately after the fire, and was completed in November 1997. There was considerable debate about the restoration of Windsor: should the damaged rooms be completely restored or replaced from scratch? Two committees were set up to supervise the work – a general Restoration Committee, chaired by the Duke of Edinburgh; and an Art and Design Committee, chaired by the Prince of Wales. In the event the damaged rooms were restored to the original George IV and Wyatville designs, but those areas which had been totally destroyed – including the old Private Chapel, the Holbein Room and the roof of St George's Hall – were rebuilt to harmonious new designs. The Sidell Gibson Partnership was chosen out of a short-list of four architects. Their aim has been to create modern Gothic, original in its detail, but continuing in a long English tradition stretching back almost without break to the Middle Ages. The Lantern Lobby is the principal new interior in the Castle. It is notable for its fine proportions and the ingenious handling of space to create interesting vistas and connections, as well as for its fine craftsmanship.

TOUR OF THE CASTLE

Visitors make their way to the State Apartments in the Upper Ward, walking past the south and west sides of the Round Tower on the steep artificial motte constructed by order of William the Conqueror. The Round Tower itself was built in stone by Henry II in 1170, and extended upwards by Wyatville in 1828–30 for George IV to improve the overall silhouette. It is an irregular oval 31.4 metres (103 feet) by 28.6 metres (94 feet) in diameter. Since 1911 it has housed the Royal Archives. The deep moat protecting the motte has always been dry, the Castle being built on a porous chalk ridge. The moat is now the well-kept garden of the Governor of the Castle, whose official residence adjoins the so-called Norman Gate.

Entrance to the State Apartments is gained from the North Terrace, which enjoys extensive views over the Thames to Eton with the picturesque outline of the fifteenth-century College Chapel and Lupton's Tower, the M4 motorway, the modern town of Slough and in the distance the wooded Buckinghamshire landscape. The white-painted domed house visible in the middle distance is Stoke Park, designed by James Wyatt for John Penn, grandson of the founder of Pennsylvania. The North Terrace was originally constructed in the sixteenth century by Henry VIII and widened by Charles II. To the east of the entrance hall is Queen Mary's Dolls' House, displayed in a specially designed room.

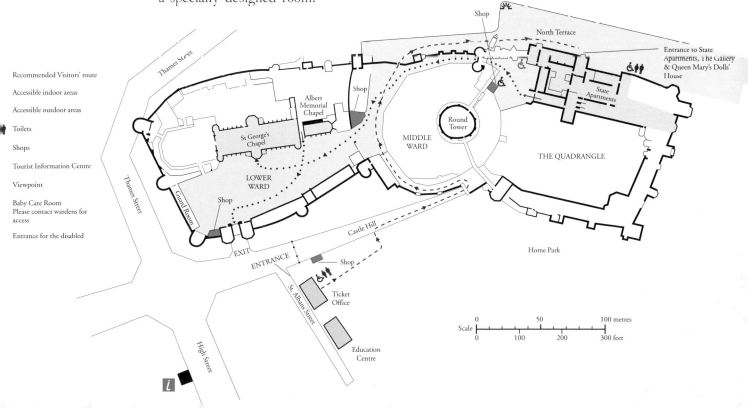

QUEEN MARY'S DOLLS' HOUSE

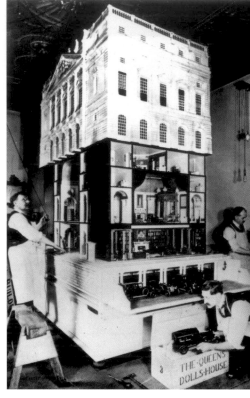

The Dolls' House was given to Queen Mary in 1924. It was designed by Sir Edwin Lutyens and nearly every item in it was specially commissioned on the tiny scale of one to twelve. It was intended as an accurate record of contemporary domestic design. The mechanical and engineering equipment – including the water system, the electric lights and the two lifts – was made to work. The gramophone plays and the bottles in the wine cellar contain genuine vintage wines.

The furniture and other contents were made by the leading manufacturers of the day. The paintings were commissioned from well-known artists and the books on the shelves of the library were written by prominent authors, some in their own hand. Rudyard Kipling, G. K. Chesterton, Sir Arthur Conan Doyle, Thomas Hardy and J. M. Barrie are among the writers represented.

On completion, the Dolls' House was shown at the British Empire Exhibition at Wembley, London, in 1924 and in the following year at the ninth Ideal Home Exhibition at Olympia, London.

In the adjoining room there is a display of the dolls named France and Marianne, with some of their remarkable trousseaux. They were presented to The Queen and Princess Margaret by the children of France in 1938.

BELOW: Detail showing the King's Bedroom

ABOVE: The Dolls' House being packed up for the 1924 Wembley Exhibition
BELOW: Detail showing the wrought-iron gates in the garden

THE GALLERY

The central vaulted undercroft, originally created by James Wyatt and extended by Jeffry Wyatville as the principal entrance to the State Apartments, was cut off when the Grand Staircase was reorientated by Queen Victoria. It now houses special exhibitions from the Royal Collection.

THE CHINA MUSEUM

The carved Ionic capitals of the columns from Hugh May's alterations for Charles II survive. In cases round the walls are displayed magnificent china services from leading English and European porcelain manufactories: Sèvres, Tournai, Meissen, Copenhagen, Naples, Rockingham and Worcester. These are still used for royal banquets and other important occasions.

DISPLAY CABINETS

(anti-clockwise from the entrance)

Royal Copenhagen dessert service presented to Edward VII and Queen Alexandra in 1863 by the ladies of Denmark

Fürstenberg service, c. 1773. Presented to George III by his brother-in-law, the Duke of Brunswick

Etruscan service, Naples, 1785–7. Presented to George III by Ferdinand IV, King of Naples, in 1787

Rockingham service, 1830–7. Commissioned by William IV in 1830

Staffordshire (Daniel) service c. 1826–30 made for the Duke of Clarence (later William IV)

Worcester service, 1830. Commissioned by William IV in 1830

Worcester harlequin service, c. 1816. Made for George IV

Coalport service, 1818. Presented to Edward, Duke of Kent, by the City of London on his marriage

Tournai service, 1787. Made for the duc d'Orléans. Acquired by George IV between 1803 and 1807

Sèvres service, 1764–70. Acquired by George IV

Group of Meissen porcelain, c. 1750

Flora Danica service, Copenhagen, 1863. Presented to Edward VII and Queen Alexandra on their wedding

ABOVE: Rockingham dessert plate

RIGHT: *Queen Victoria and Napoleon III in the State Entrance*, by G. Thomas, 1855

THE GRAND STAIRCASE

This is the third staircase to the main floor since the restoration of the Castle was begun by George III in the late eighteenth century. James Wyatt constructed a staircase in the space now occupied by the Grand Vestibule. Wyatville removed it and built a new staircase on the present site, by roofing over the medieval Brick Court. This arrangement, in turn, was considered inconvenient and the present staircase on a reversed alignment was contrived by Anthony Salvin in 1866.

The staircase is filled with light from a glazed timber lantern carried on four stone arches. The walls are lined with trophies of arms which perpetuate arrangements originally worked out by Sir Samuel Rush Meyrick, who was knighted by William IV for his work. The large marble statue of George IV on the half-landing survives from Wyatville's design and commemorates the monarch who is largely responsible for the present appearance of Windsor Castle. It was carved by Sir Francis Chantrey in 1828–32.

RIGHT: The Grand
Staircase

THE GRAND STAIRCASE AND THE GRAND VESTIBULE

THE GRAND STAIRCASE

SCULPTURE

1   Over-life size statue of George IV by Sir Francis Chantrey, 1828–32. Copied at the King's request from Chantrey's bronze statue at Brighton

ARMS & ARMOUR

2   Colours of disbanded Irish and English regiments

3   Trophies and suits of armour, 16th–19th centuries

4   Boy's armour made for Henry, Prince of Wales, Greenwich, c. 1610

5   Boy's armour made for Henry, Prince of Wales, probably French, c. 1610

THE GRAND VESTIBULE

PICTURES

1   David Morier, *George II on Horseback*, c. 1745

2   John Vanderbank, *George I on Horseback*, 1726

FURNITURE

3   Range of fitted oak cases, made to display Queen Victoria's Golden Jubilee presents, 1887–9. Later rearranged to display Oriental and European arms, relics, etc

ARMS & ARMOUR

4   Arms and armour and relics of Tipu Sultan, King of Mysore,

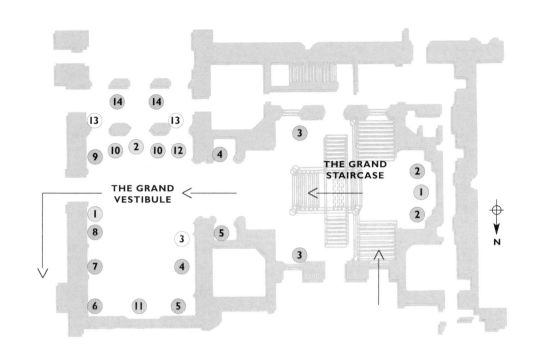

including the gold tiger from his throne, taken at Seringapatam in 1799

5   Oriental arms and trophies including an Inca crown and an Ethiopian crown, c 1840

6   European firearms including sporting guns, mainly 18th century

7   Trophy of swords, European, 17th–18th centuries, and a damascened iron round target or shield, Paris or Antwerp, mid-16th century

8   European arms including French pistols and a sword by N–N. Boutet; the travelling service of Stephanie Beauharnais, by Biennais, Paris, 1798–1809; Napoleon's scarlet cloak, captured at Waterloo; and the bullet that

killed Lord Nelson at Trafalgar, 1805

9   Three embroidered velvet cloaks and a surcoat and stole made for George IV, reputedly used at the Hanoverian Coronation in 1821, and a group of sabretaches and pouches from Hussar regiments

SCULPTURE

10   Marble busts of Charles I and William III, early 18th century. Acquired by Queen Elizabeth in 1937

11   Marble statue of Queen Victoria with her collie Sharp, by Sir J. E. Boehm, 1871

12   Bronze plaque representing Rudolph II introducing the Liberal Arts into Bohemia, by Adrian de Vries, 1609. Purchased by George IV

THE LOBBY TO THE GRAND VESTIBULE

FURNITURE

13   Two leather-covered sedan chairs with gilt metal decoration, late 18th century. Belonged to Queen Charlotte. Acquired by Queen Victoria in 1883 from the Duke of Teck. The chair on the right by William Griffin

ARMS & ARMOUR

14   Two cases containing equipment of the 10th Light Dragoons including a jacket and helmet belonging to George IV as Colonel of the Regiment (1793–1819)

THE GRAND VESTIBULE

The lantern and vaulting date from George III's reign. The arms and relics include the bullet that killed Nelson, and a gold tiger from the throne of Tipu, Sultan of Mysore.

THE GRAND VESTIBULE

For plan see page 15

This was the top of James Wyatt's staircase. When first built, the central lantern was 30 metres (100 feet) above floor level. The handsome plaster fan vault, with naturalistic foliage bosses and angels, was executed by Francis Bernasconi, a plasterer of genius who first worked at Windsor under James Wyatt, but continued under Wyatville. The glazed Gothic showcases round the sides of the room were made in 1888 to display Queen Victoria's Golden Jubilee presents. They now

BELOW: The Grand Vestibule

contain a collection of arms, including trophies from the conquest of Seringapatam in India in 1799 and the Napoleonic Wars – not least the lead bullet that killed Nelson at Trafalgar in 1805. The room is dominated by a statue of Queen Victoria by Joseph Boehm (1871).

ABOVE: Golden tiger's head from the throne of Tipu Sultan

BELOW: The bullet which killed Nelson

16

THE ANTE THRONE ROOM

This small room is much reduced from its seventeenth-century dimensions; then it was the King's Audience Chamber. Here stood the King's chair of state until the reign of George III. Wyatville reduced it in size and turned it into an ante-room. Today it marks the approximate divide between that part of the Castle remodelled in the reign of George IV to make larger and grander reception rooms, and Charles II's smaller State Apartments. The latter still retain their old layout and proportions and some of their seventeenth-century character and architectural detail, though Wyatville replaced all except three of Verrio's painted ceilings on the grounds that they were irreparably decayed.

The room has recently been restored and hung with green damask. The carved oak cornice decorated with acanthus leaves alone survives from Grinling Gibbons' work for Charles II.

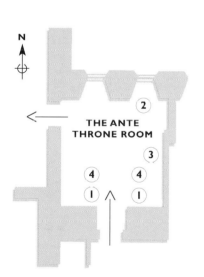

FURNITURE

1 Pair of giltwood mirrors (originally picture frames) carved with the cyphers of William III and Mary II

2 Rosewood and brass-inlaid centre table, early-19th century

3 Settee and chairs by Morel & Seddon, c. 1828

4 Pair of ebony and Boulle marquetry side cabinets, mid 19th century

---

THE ANTE THRONE ROOM

This was Charles II's Audience Chamber, and in the seventeenth and eighteenth centuries it contained the King's chair of state. It was much reduced in size by Sir Jeffry Wyatville, as part of George IV's alterations.

THE WATERLOO CHAMBER

The visitor passes through this vast room, created by Wyatville by roofing over the former Horn Court, on the way to the King's and Queen's State Apartments. It was designed to display Sir Thomas Lawrence's portraits of the Allied leaders responsible for the defeat of Napoleon.

There is an opportunity to inspect the room and the pictures in more detail later in the tour; see page 59.

THE KING'S DRAWING ROOM

This was the third room in the King's State Apartments. It and the following rooms are Charles II's additions to the Castle, partly redecorated in the late eighteenth and early nineteenth centuries. In the nineteenth century this and the adjoining rooms were all occupied as a suite by state visitors, but they have been superseded by more comfortable bedrooms on the south side of the Castle. Today they are mainly used for the display of works of art from the Royal Collection.

ABOVE: *The Holy Family with St Francis,* by Rubens, 1626–8

In the nineteenth century the King's Drawing Room was known as the Rubens Room from the paintings by Rubens and his school which still hang here today. Prince Albert developed the theme of hanging particular groups of paintings in particular rooms, which the visitor will note while going round the State Apartments. Wyatville's geometrical plaster ceiling is embellished with the arms of George IV and the Garter Star. Sadly, it replaces one of Verrio's most ambitious paintings, showing Charles II triumphant in a chariot, scattering his enemies. It was one of a series of thirteen painted ceilings that celebrated the Restoration of the English monarchy in 1660. They all had fulsomely Royalist subjects, and were influenced by Charles Lebrun's work for Louis XIV at Versailles.

The seventeenth-century carved cornice by Grinling Gibbons with its crisply carved acanthus leaves survives, as do the panelled dado and 8-panelled doors. George III replaced the oak wall panels with bright damask. In his time it was Garter blue; George IV changed it to crimson. Now it is yellow. The early

BELOW: The Garter Star and monogram of George IV from the cornice

BELOW: The King's Drawing Room

ABOVE: *Winter*, by Rubens, 1620–30

nineteenth-century Siena marble chimneypiece was designed by Wyatville, who also added the large bay window from which there is a good view over Eton. George IV's body lay in state in this room after his death in 1830. Queen Victoria often used the room for private theatrical performances, a temporary stage being erected in the window bay.

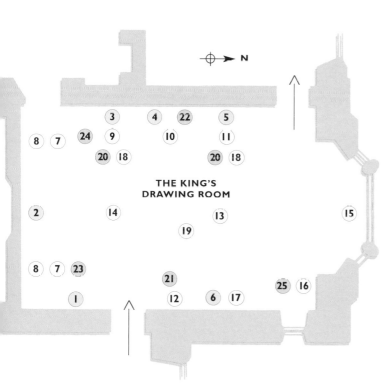

THE KING'S
DRAWING ROOM

PICTURES

1 Studio of Sir Peter Paul Rubens, *Equestrian Portrait of Philip II of Spain*, c. 1620

2 Studio of Sir Peter Paul Rubens, *Portrait of a Gentleman on Horseback*, c. 1610

3 Sir Peter Paul Rubens, *Winter: Interior of a Barn*, 1620–30

4 Sir Peter Paul Rubens, *The Holy Family with St Francis*, 1626–8 (overmantel)

5 Sir Peter Paul Rubens, *Summer: Landscape with Peasants Going to Market*, 1620–30

6 Sir Anthony Van Dyck, *St Martin Dividing his Cloak*, c. 1618–20

FURNITURE

7 Pair of Boulle and lacquer cabinets, 18th and 19th centuries

8 Two oval carved and giltwood pier glasses designed by John Yenn, c. 1794–5, and carved by Richard Lawrence

9 French lacquer and gilt bronze cabinet, late 18th and 19th centuries

10 Pair of English giltwood torchères, c. 1730

11 French lacquer and gilt bronze cabinet by J. Baumhauer, c. 1770. Acquired by George IV in 1825

12 Set of four Baroque giltwood torchères, c. 1840

13 French ebony and Boulle marquetry writing table, c. 1710

14 Giltwood seat furniture by Morel & Seddon, c. 1828

15 Organ-clock by Charles Clay, c. 1730, incorporating a rock crystal and enamelled casket by Melchior Baumgartner, Augsburg, 1664, containing the Bible of General Gordon of Khartoum

16 French ebony and lacquer secretaire, late 18th century

17 French ebony veneered writing desk, late 18th century

18 Pair of 18th-century gilt bronze allegorical groups representing Painting and Sculpture. Purchased by George IV in 1827

19 Persian carpet, early 20th century. Presented to King Edward VII by the Shah of Persia in 1903

PORCELAIN

20 Four Chinese blue and white porcelain jars and covers, 17th century

21 Four candelabra of Chinese blue porcelain with French gilt bronze mounts, 18th century

22 Pair of Chinese celadon porcelain vases, mid-18th century

SCULPTURE

23 Bronze equestrian group of *Marcus Aurelius* after the Antique, 18th century

24 Bronze equestrian group of *Henri IV*, 18th century

25 Bronze figure of *Hercules* after Giambologna, ?18th century

THE KING'S DRAWING ROOM

There is a splendid view over Eton from Wyatville's bay window. George IV's body lay in state in this room after his death. The paintings by Rubens include the distinguished *Holy Family with St Francis* (over the fireplace) and two landscapes.

THE KING'S BED CHAMBER

Georgia III removed the seventeenth-century wainscot from the walls and hung them with crimson cloth (most recently renewed in damask). Wyatville replaced Verrio's painted ceiling of Charles II receiving homage with a plaster composition incorporating the Stuart royal arms and the date 1660 to commemorate the Restoration, but kept Grinling Gibbons' excellent

carved cornice. The white marble chimneypiece, designed by Sir William Chambers, was brought from Buckingham House. The bed, attributed to the French cabinet-maker Georges Jacob, was acquired by George IV. It was given its present hangings of green and purple for the State Visit of the Emperor Napoleon III in 1855. His initials and those of the Empress Eugénie are embroidered on the foot of the bed. The Emperor was invested with the Order of the Garter by Queen Victoria while he was at Windsor.

ABOVE: *Venice: The Bacino di S. Marco on Ascension Day*, by Canaletto, c. 1733-4

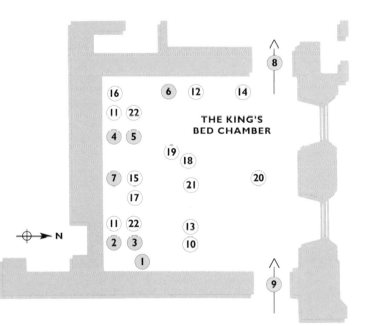

THE KING'S BED CHAMBER

FURNITURE

10 French giltwood 'polonaise' bed attributed to G. Jacob, late 18th century. The hangings incorporate 18th- and 19th-century needlework, the latter made for the State Visit of Emperor Napoleon III and Empress Eugénie in 1855

11 Pair of English marquetry cabinets with gilt bronze mounts, attributed to P. Langlois, mid-18th century

12 English serpentine mahogany cabinet with gilt bronze mounts, c. 1760

13 French oval parquetry table by R. Lacroix, c. 1770, inset with Sèvres porcelain plaque dated 1763

14 Gilt gesso side chairs, c. 1730

15 Gilt bronze, white marble and Derby porcelain temple clock by Vulliamy, c. 1790

16 Gilt bronze and white marble allegorical clock with Derby porcelain figure by Vulliamy, 1787, on satinwood pedestal

17 Pair of French white marble and gilt bronze vases, late 18th century

18 Regency rosewood games table, early 19th century

19 Mahogany trellis-back chair by G. Jacob, late 18th century

20 French (Savonnerie) carpet, second half of 18th century

21 Cut-glass chandelier, early 19th century

22 Pair of French patinated and gilt bronze candelabra by F. Rémond, made in 1783 for the comte d'Artois at Versailles. Acquired by George IV

PICTURES

1 Francis Cotes, *Queen Charlotte with Charlotte, Princess Royal*, 1767

2 Canaletto, *Venice: Caprice View of the Piazzetta with the Horses of S. Marco*, 1743

3 Canaletto, *Venice: A Regatta on the Grand Canal*, c. 1733

4 Canaletto, *Venice: The Colleoni Monument in a Caprice Setting*, 1744

5 Canaletto, *Venice: The Bacino di S. Marco on Ascension Day*, c. 1733–4

6 Thomas Gainsborough, *John Hayes St Leger*, 1782

7 Thomas Gainsborough, *Johann Christian Fischer*, c. 1780 (overmantel)

Over doors

8 Canaletto, *Venice: Caprice View of the Molo and the Doge's Palace*, c. 1743

9 Canaletto, *Venice: Caprice View of the Courtyard of the Doge's Palace with the Scala dei Giganti*, 1744

THE KING'S BED CHAMBER

In the nineteenth century this was used by visiting monarchs on state visits. The bed bears the embroidered initials of Napoleon III and Empress Eugénie. The marble fireplace was brought from Buckingham House. The paintings include several Canalettos purchased by George III and two full-length Gainsborough portraits.

THE KING'S DRESSING ROOM

This room, though not large, makes up for its small scale in the superb quality of the paintings hanging in it. It is arranged as a picture cabinet and contains some of the finest small masterpieces in the Royal Collection, including portraits by Holbein, Dürer, Memling, Rubens and Rembrandt. Over the fireplace hangs Van Dyck's famous portrait of Charles I from three angles. This was painted to send to Bernini in Rome, to assist him in carving a marble bust of the King. The

BELOW: The King's Dressing Room (detail)

ABOVE: *Twelfth Night Feast*, by Jan Steen, c. 1665

BELOW: *Henrietta Maria*, by Sir Anthony Van Dyck, c. 1632

bust itself was lost in the fire that destroyed Whitehall Palace in 1698. The carved wooden cornice by Grinling Gibbons and the panelled dado survive from the time of Charles II. Here, as in the other state rooms, the walls were stripped of wainscot and hung with crimson cloth by George III. William IV eliminated the old painted ceiling and installed the existing moulded plaster design sporting his own monogram and arms, while the anchors and tridents recall his career in the Navy before he ascended the throne. The handsome white marble chimneypiece was brought from Queen Charlotte's Breakfast Room at Buckingham House. King Charles II actually slept in this room rather than in his state bedroom next door, which he used for the official ceremony of levée (rising, resting and receiving) and private business.

ABOVE: *An Old Woman: 'The Artist's Mother'*, by Rembrandt, c. 1629

PICTURES

1 Albrecht Dürer, *Portrait of a Young Man*, 1506

2 Hans Memling, *Portrait of a Man*, c. 1478–80

3 Sir Anthony Van Dyck, *Charles I in Three Positions*, c. 1635–6

4 Jean Clouet, *Portrait of a Man Holding a Volume of Petrarch*, c. 1530

5 Hans Holbein the Younger, *William Reskimer*, c. 1532–3

6 Adriaen van de Velde the Elder, *Figures on the Coast at Scheveningen*, 1660

7 Rembrandt van Rijn, *Self Portrait*, 1642

8 Sir Peter Paul Rubens, *Portrait of the Artist*, 1622

9 Gerrit van Honthorst, *Princess Sophia, Electress of Hanover*, c. 1650

10 Sir Peter Paul Rubens, *Portrait of a Lady*, 1625–30

11 Sir Peter Paul Rubens, *Portrait of Sir Anthony Van Dyck*, 1627–8

12 Jan Steen, *Twelfth Night Feast: The King Drinks*, c. 1665

13 Rembrandt van Rijn, *A Young Man Wearing a Turban*, 1631

14 Nicholaes Berchem, *Italian Landscape with Figures and Animals: A Village on a Plateau*, 1655

15 Sir Anthony Van Dyck, *Henrietta Maria*, c. 1632

16 Rembrandt van Rijn, *An Old Woman: 'The Artist's Mother'*, c. 1629

17 Cornelis van Poelenburgh, *Shepherds with Their Flocks in a Landscape with Ruins*, c. 1620

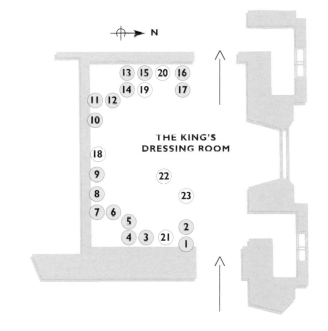

N

THE KING'S DRESSING ROOM

FURNITURE

18 French Boulle marquetry bureau, c. 1680. Probably made for the duchesse de Retz

19 English Boulle marquetry cabinet, attributed to Gerrit Jensen, c. 1695. Made for William III and Mary II

20 French mahogany trellis-back chairs by G. Jacob, late 18th century

21 Pair of French gilt bronze perfume burners, early 19th century

22 English gilt bronze chandelier in the style of Louis XIV, early 19th century

23 Persian silk and wool carpet, late 19th century

THE KING'S DRESSING ROOM

King Charles II slept here rather than in his state bedroom next door. The portraits include several masterpieces: Van Dyck's *Triple Portrait of Charles I*, Rembrandt's *'The Artist's Mother'* and Rubens' *Self Portrait*.

THE KING'S CLOSET

his was created out of two smaller rooms by James Wyatt in 1804. Here again the seventeenth-century cornice and dado survive (or have been copied), but the wall panels gave way to more cheerful hangings in the reign of George III and the present ceiling is of moulded plaster to Wyatville's design. It is dated 1833 and displays the monogram and arms of Adelaide of Saxe-Meiningen, Queen Consort of King William IV.

LEFT: The King's Closet

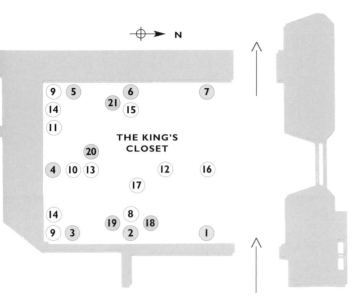

THE KING'S
CLOSET

FURNITURE

8 French lacquer cabinet with gilt bronze mounts, c. 1775 and later

9 Pair of French corner cupboards with Japanese lacquer panels and gilt bronze mounts, by Bernard (II) van Risamburgh, c. 1750

10 French chest of drawers with Japanese lacquer panels and gilt bronze mounts, by Bernard (II) van Risamburgh, c. 1750

11 French mahogany trellis-back chairs by G. Jacob, late 18th century

12 English mahogany and satinwood writing-table, c. 1800

13 French patinated and gilt bronze 'Rape of Europa' clock, case by R. Osmond, later movement by B. L. Vulliamy, on musical box base, mid-18th century

14 Pair of celadon porcelain and gilt bronze candelabra by the Vulliamys, 1819

15 French patinated and gilt bronze mantel clock, movement by Vulliamy, mid 18th century

16 Persian wool and silk carpet, 19th century

17 English gilt bronze chandelier, c. 1830

PORCELAIN

18 Pair of celadon porcelain vases with French gilt bronze mounts, late 18th century

19 Celadon porcelain vase with French gilt bronze mounts, mid-18th century

20 Pair of celadon porcelain vases and covers with French gilt bronze mounts, early 18th century

21 Pair of celadon porcelain vases with French gilt bronze mounts, mid-18th century

PICTURES

1 Allan Ramsay, *Prince William, later Duke of Clarence*, c. 1767

2 Sir Joshua Reynolds, *Francis Rawdon-Hastings, 2nd Earl of Moira and 1st Marquis of Hastings*, 1789–90

3 John Hoppner, *John Willett Payne*, c. 1800

4 Canaletto, *Venice: The Grand Canal with S. Maria Della Salute*, 1744

5 Richard Brompton, *Edward, Duke of York, with his Friends in Venice*, 1763

6 John Hoppner, *George Keith Elphinstone, later Viscount Keith*, c. 1800

7 Johann Zoffany, *The Lens Maker John Cuff*, 1772

RIGHT: *John Cuff*, by Johann Zoffany, 1772

FAR RIGHT: *Prince William, later Duke of Clarence*, by Ramsay, c. 1767

THE KING'S CLOSET

The English eighteenth-century portraits include a splendid late Reynolds full length of the 2nd Earl of Moira, and *Prince William, later Duke of Clarence* by Ramsay.

THE QUEEN'S DRAWING ROOM

As at Hampton Court, the King and Queen's State Apartments adjoin at right angles. All the Queen's apartments survive, except the bed chamber which is now part of the adjoining Royal Library (not open to the public). The visitor sees them in reverse order. The Queen's Drawing Room was originally hung with tapestry

BELOW: The Queen's
Drawing Room

PICTURES

1 Adriaen Hanneman, *Mary, Princess of Orange*, c. 1655

2 Hans Holbein the Younger, *Sir Henry Guildford*, 1527

3 After Hans Holbein the Younger, *Henry VIII*, c. 1545

4 Hans Holbein the Younger, *Derich Born*, 1533

5 Hans Holbein the Younger, *Thomas Howard, 3rd Duke of Norfolk*, 1538–9

6 Robert Peake the Elder, *Henry, Prince of Wales, in the Hunting Field*, c. 1605

7 Anon., British School, *Edward VI*, 1546–7

8 After Anthonis Mor, *Mary I*, c. 1575

9 Hans Holbein the Younger, *A Merchant of the German Steelyard: 'Hans of Antwerp'*, 1532

10 Anon., British School, *Elizabeth I, when Princess*, c. 1546

11 Willem Wissing, *William III*, c. 1685

12 Paul van Somer, *James I*, c. 1620

13 John Riley, *Prince George of Denmark*, 1687

14 John Riley, *Bridget Holmes*, 1686

15 Willem Wissing, *Mary II*, 1685

16 Studio of Sir Anthony Van Dyck, *Mary, Princess of Orange*, c. 1641

17 William Dobson, *Charles II, when Prince of Wales*, 1644

18 Leonard Knyff, *A View of the North Front of Windsor Castle*, c. 1705

19 Sir Peter Lely, *Mary II, when Princess*, c. 1672

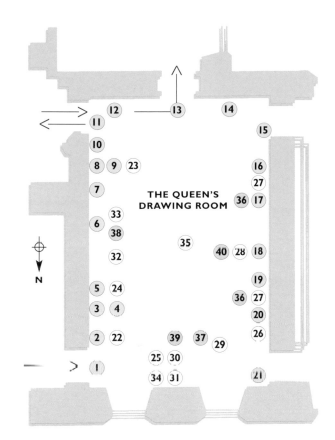

20 Adriaen Hanneman, *William III, when Prince of Orange*, 1664

21 Simon Verelst, *Mary of Modena, Duchess of York*, c. 1675

FURNITURE

22 English walnut and seaweed marquetry bureau, late 17th century

23 French floral marquetry pedestal bureau, late 17th century

24 Pair of English giltwood candle stands, c. 1740. Purchased by Queen Elizabeth in 1947. Formerly at Ditchley Park

25 Astronomical clock by Jakob Mayr, Augsburg, late 17th century

26 English gilt gesso chairs, c. 1730 and later

27 Pair of English giltwood side tables with marble tops, late 18th century

28 French ebony cabinet-on-stand, carved with scenes from contemporary literature, c. 1650

29 Ebony and giltwood centre table by Morel & Seddon, c. 1828

30 Giltwood pier table with scagliola top, by Marsh & Tatham, 1814. Made for Carlton House

31 English giltwood pier glass, early 19th century

32 Pair of French marble and gilt bronze candelabra, late 18th century

33 French gilt bronze mantel clock, case by R. Osmond, movement by J. Lepaute, c. 1780

34 Pair of rouge marble and gilt bronze candelabra, late 18th century

35 English gilt bronze chandelier by Hancock & Rixon, 1828

PORCELAIN

36 Pair of Chinese blue porcelain candelabra with French and English mounts, 18th and 19th centuries

37 Chinese *famille rose* punch bowl, mid-18th century

38 Pair of Chinese blue and gold porcelain vases and covers with French gilt bronze mounts, early 18th century

39 Chinese blue porcelain cistern with French gilt bronze mounts, mid-18th century. Possibly belonged to Mme de Pompadour

40 Pair of Chinese white porcelain vases, presented to Queen Victoria for her Diamond Jubilee (1897) by the Emperor of China

ABOVE: *James I*, by Paul van Somer, c. 1620

THE QUEEN'S DRAWING ROOM
The Queen's state rooms adjoined the King's. Holbein's portrait of Sir Henry Guildford displayed here is among the artist's finest works. The gilt bronze chandelier was commissioned by George IV for the Castle.

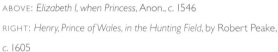

ABOVE: *Elizabeth I, when Princess,* Anon., c. 1546

RIGHT: *Henry, Prince of Wales, in the Hunting Field,* by Robert Peake,
c. 1605

and Verrio's ceiling was painted with an assembly of the gods. In 1834
Wyatville remodelled the room, except the dado and cornice, to match
the King's rooms for William IV. His plaster ceiling with its broad
mouldings and naturalistic foliage was intended to create a neo-
Caroline effect. The arms are those of King William IV and Queen
Adelaide. The large panes of glass in the windows are among the
earliest plate glass in England. The white marble chimneypiece was
commissioned by George III, but is not in its original position. Now displayed here are some of the finest sixteenth- and seventeenth-century
English portraits in the Royal Collection, including four by Holbein.

The visitor makes a detour from the Queen's apartments,
through the Octagon Lobby, to the King's Dining Room.

THE OCTAGON LOBBY

This has oak panels and reset Gibbons carvings, including splendid
oval reliefs of the heads of saints from the old Royal Chapel.

THE KING'S DINING ROOM

ABOVE: Details of the
ceiling frieze

OVERLEAF: The King's
Dining Room

This room retains much of its Charles II character, though it was modified by Salvin when he rebuilt the adjoining Grand Staircase; he inserted the skylights over the alcoves, which were originally closets for musicians and servants. It is now rather dark but originally the room was lit by windows into the Brick Court. Verrio's ceiling survives here; it depicts a banquet of the gods. The still lifes of fruit, fish and fowl in the coving are particularly attractive; note the lobster. The magnificent wood carvings are by Grinling Gibbons and his assistant Henry Phillips, but were not all originally in this room; the palm fronds over the alcoves, for instance, were in the Chapel. In this room Charles II dined in public on certain days, as did Louis XIV at Versailles. At the end of the meal he withdrew to the adjoining King's Drawing Room.

This room owes something of its present appearance to Queen Mary, consort of George V, who in the early twentieth century oversaw the restoration of the State Apartments. Here, she replaced the oak wainscot and installed the two Brussels tapestries with the arms of William III. Other pieces from this set are at Het Loo, William III's palace in Holland.

BELOW: *Michael Alphonsus Shen Fu-Tsung. The Chinese Convert*', by Sir Godfrey Kneller, 1687

THE KING'S DINING ROOM

PICTURES

1 Jacob Huysmans, *Catherine of Braganza*, 1664 (overmantel)

2 Sir Godfrey Kneller, *Michael Alphonsus Shen Fu-Tsung. 'The Chinese Convert'*, 1687

3 Studio of Philippe de Champaigne, *Louis XIII, King of France*, c. 1630

FURNITURE

4 French ebony and Boulle marquetry secretaire, the base c. 1710, the upper part c. 1770, by E. Levasseur. Bought by George IV in 1812

5 Pair of English giltwood torchères, c. 1730

6 Ebony and Boulle marquetry breakfront cabinet, early 19th century

7 Pair of English giltwood pier glasses, c. 1740

8 Cedarwood and marquetry drop-front cabinet (vargueño), Spanish (?), late 16th century and later

9 French Boulle marquetry pedestal clock, late 17th century, with 19th-century movement by B. L. Vulliamy. Purchased by George IV in 1820

10 Pair of giltwood pier tables attributed to Jean Pelletier, c. 1699

11 Pair of English giltwood pier glasses with cypher of Queen Anne, early 18th century and later

12 English walnut and floral marquetry side table, late 17th century

13 English walnut and seaweed marquetry side table, late 17th century

14 Giltwood pier table with cypher of Queen Anne, early 18th century

15 Ebony medicine cabinet with silver gilt mounts, Augsburg, early 17th century, on a later stand

16 Group of caned walnut chairs, late 17th century

17 Boulle marquetry mantel clock, late 17th century, with 19th-century movement by B. L. Vulliamy

18 Ebony bracket clock by Thomas Tompion, late 17th century

19 Collection of Chinese jade carvings, 18th–19th centuries

20 English needlework casket, c. 1680

21 English silver-mounted marquetry bellows, late 17th century. Traditionally belonged to Nell Gwyn

22 Japanese lacquer casket, late 17th century

23 Six gilt metal wall sconces with cypher of Charles II, 19th century

TAPESTRIES

24 Two Brussels panels with the arms of William III and Mary II, designed by Daniel Marot, c. 1700. Purchased by Queen Mary in 1914

PORCELAIN

25 Two pairs of Chinese porcelain *famille verte* baluster vases, 17th century

26 Group of Japanese Arita porcelain 'Hampton Court' vases and square bottles, c. 1700, some with 18th-century French gilt bronze mounts

27 Japanese Arita porcelain baluster vase, c. 1700, with later French gilt bronze mounts

28 Pair of Chinese porcelain long-necked bottles, c. 1700

SCULPTURE

29 Limewood festoons and drops by Grinling Gibbons and workshop, 1676–7

30 Terracotta bust of Charles II, late 17th century

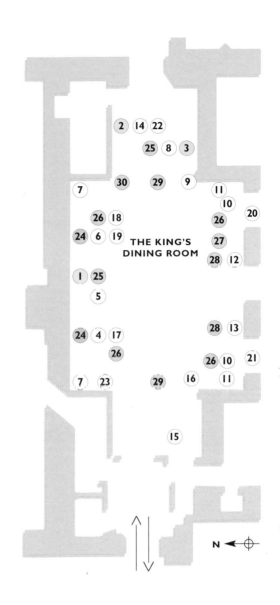

THE KING'S
DINING ROOM

N

THE KING'S DINING ROOM

Charles II dined in public in this room. Verrio's ceiling is one of only three to survive out of the thirteen he painted for the Castle. The room is also decorated with Grinling Gibbons carvings.

THE QUEEN'S BALLROOM

Returning to the Queen's rooms, we reach the ballroom or Queen's Gallery, extensively remodelled by Wyatville for William IV. During a State Visit to Windsor Castle, the visiting Head of State receives members of the Diplomatic Corps here. It retains a Charles II dado and carved cornice. The white marble chimneypiece, one of George III's, was brought from the Queen's Bed Chamber when the latter was converted into part of the Royal Library. The

three magnificent glass chandeliers, also commissioned by George III, are among the finest English examples. Since the nineteenth century the room has also been known as the Van Dyck Room; it is hung entirely with portraits by him. The silver furniture here is a very rare survival of the grandest seventeenth-century royal taste. Comparable examples now exist at Knole in Kent and Rosenborg Castle in Copenhagen. All Louis XIV's silver furniture at Versailles, which inspired the fashion, was melted down towards the end of his reign to pay for his European wars.

ABOVE: *The Five Eldest Children of Charles I*, by Van Dyck, 1637

LEFT: The Queen's Ballroom

THE QUEEN'S BALLROOM

PICTURES

1 Sir Anthony Van Dyck, *Charles I in Robes of State*, 1636

2 Sir Anthony Van Dyck, *Portrait of a Woman*, c. 1634–5

3 Sir Anthony Van Dyck, *Thomas Killigrew and William, Lord Crofts (?)*, 1638

4 Sir Anthony Van Dyck, *George Villiers, 2nd Duke of Buckingham, and Lord Francis Villiers*, 1635

5 Sir Anthony Van Dyck, *Lady Mary Villiers, Duchess of Richmond, as St Agnes*, c. 1637

6 Sir Anthony Van Dyck, *The Three Eldest Children of Charles I*, 1635

7 Sir Anthony Van Dyck, *Beatrice of Cusance, Princess of Cantecroix and Duchess of Lorraine*, c. 1635

8 Sir Anthony Van Dyck, *The Five Eldest Children of Charles I*, 1637

FURNITURE

9 Pair of English Boulle marquetry writing tables by Louis Le Gaigneur. Purchased by George IV in 1815

10 Pair of French corner cupboards with Japanese lacquer panels and

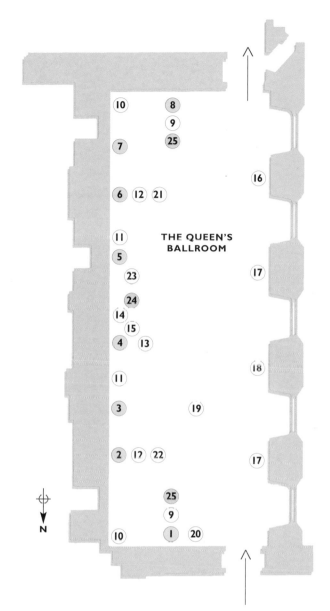

gilt bronze mounts, mid-18th century. Purchased by George IV in 1829

11 French giltwood seat furniture by G. Jacob, c. 1785. Supplied by Dominique Daguerre for the Prince of Wales at Carlton House

12 Two ebony cabinets with Japanese lacquer panels, one (on right)

The Negress Head Clock, by J-A. Lépine, 1790

French, c. 1770; the other made to match by Morel & Hughes, 1812

13 Pair of English Boulle marquetry octagonal tables by T. Parker. Given to George IV by Queen Charlotte

14 English silver mirror, c. 1670

15 French gilt bronze mantel clock by J-A. Lépine, 1790. Purchased by

George IV in that year. The time is indicated in the negress's eyeballs. The base contains a small organ which is controlled by pulling one of the earrings

16 English cast silver pier table and mirror by Andrew Moore, c. 1695. Presented to William III by the Corporation of the City of London

17 Pair of cabinets veneered with cocus wood and with silver mounts, c. 1665. Probably made for Queen Henrietta Maria. Presented to King George V by Lord Rothschild, 1910

18 Repoussé silver pier glass, table and pair of candlestands, c. 1670. Presented to Charles II by the Corporation of the City of London

19 Set of three English cut glass chandeliers, c. 1800

20 Seven silver sconces, repoussé with Garter badges, c. 1680

21 Pair of green marble vases and a porphyry vase, with French gilt bronze mounts, c. 1780

22 Garniture of porphyry vases with gilt bronze mounts, c. 1780

23 Pair of French Boulle marquetry torchères with gilt bronze mounts, c. 1700

PORCELAIN

24 Pair of Wedgwood jasperware, gilt bronze and cut glass candelabra, c. 1780

25 Pair of porcelain tureens and covers with gilt bronze mounts, 19th century

> ## THE QUEEN'S BALLROOM
> The silver furniture, along the window side, is a very rare survival of seventeenth-century royal taste. The portraits by Van Dyck include Charles I's children.

33

THE QUEEN'S AUDIENCE CHAMBER

This room and the adjoining Presence Chamber are the best-preserved survivors from Charles II's time, and give an idea of the appearance of all the State Apartments as remodelled for him by Hugh May and his team of brilliant craftsmen. Verrio's painted ceiling shows Catherine of Braganza (wife of Charles II) being drawn in a chariot by swans towards a temple of

LEFT: The Queen's Audience Chamber

THE QUEEN'S AUDIENCE CHAMBER
The Baroque decoration survives from Charles II's time. The Verrio ceiling depicts his wife, Catherine of Braganza, in a triumphal chariot.

virtue, while the cove is treated as a *faux* balustrade. The general form of the ceiling is inspired by Le Brun's work at Versailles. The cornice, carved with acanthus leaves, and the festoons of fruit and flowers framing portraits in the overdoors are by Grinling Gibbons, Henry Phillips and their assistants. Though inspired by Louis XIV's palace interiors, the use of wainscot and wood carvings rather than marbles gives the Windsor rooms a different character. The general appearance of the room with oak wainscot framing tapestries recalls the original appearance of the Queen's Drawing Room, though these particular tapestries were acquired for George IV in Paris in 1825. In the seventeenth century the Queen's chair of state stood here under a canopy. The chimney-piece, by William Kent, was brought from St James's in the early nineteenth century to replace one with a plain bolection moulding.

ABOVE: *Mary, Queen of Scots*, Anon, c. 1620

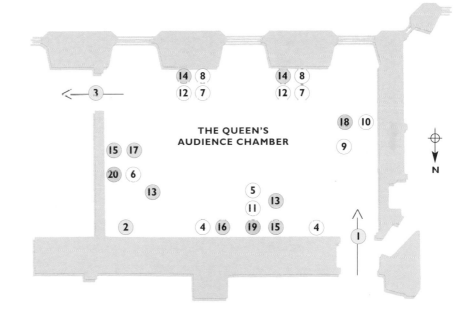

PICTURES

Over doors

1 Gerrit van Honthorst, *William II, Prince of Orange*, c. 1640

2 Gerrit van Honthorst, *Frederick Henry, Prince of Orange*, 1631

3 Anon., British School, *Mary, Queen of Scots*, c. 1620

FURNITURE

4 Two Chinese lacquer cabinets, late 17th century, on English giltwood tables, c. 1740

5 Giltwood firescreen with Beauvais tapestry panel by Michel Vellaud, 1815

6 Flemish ebony cabinet-on-stand with gilt bronze mounts, late 17th century and later

7 Pair of English giltwood pier tables, c. 1760. Purchased by Queen Mary in 1932. Formerly at Chesterfield House

8 Pair of English giltwood pier glasses, early 19th century

9 Ebony cabinet with *pietra dura* panels of flowers and dwarfs, by

A.-L. Bellangé, c. 1820. Purchased by George IV in 1825

10 English gilt gesso chairs, c. 1730 and later

11 Patinated and gilt bronze mantel clock with palm tree and figures, by Justin Vulliamy, late 18th century

12 Pair of bronze lamps by the Vulliamys, c. 1810. Purchased by George IV for Carlton House

PORCELAIN

13 Pair of English giltwood x-frame armchairs attributed to Henry Williams, 1737

14 Two pairs of Japanese Imari porcelain vases and covers, late 17th century

15 Two pairs of large Chinese blue and white vases and covers, c. 1700

16 Pair of French white porcelain and gilt bronze candelabra, late 18th century

17 Garniture of three Delft pottery vases and covers, c. 1700

TAPESTRIES

Three Gobelins panels from the History of Esther after J.-F. de Troy, woven by Audran and Cozette, 1779–87, purchased by George IV in 1825

18 *The Coronation of Esther*

19 *The Triumph of Mordecai*

20 *The Toilette of Esther*

THE QUEEN'S PRESENCE CHAMBER

BELOW: The Queen's
Presence Chamber

This is an even more splendid example of Hugh May's work than the Audience Chamber. Verrio's ceiling shows Catherine of Braganza seated under a canopy held by zephyrs while figures of Envy and Sedition retreat before the out-stretched Sword of Justice. The cornice and carved festoons of the overmantel and overdoors are further demonstrations of the genius of the English seventeenth-century school of wood carvers. The large

THE QUEEN'S PRESENCE CHAMBER

marble chimneypiece incorporates a clock flanked by reclining figures of Vigilance and Patience. It was carved by John Bacon R.A. in 1789 and was originally made for the Saloon at Buckingham House. The Gobelins tapestries were acquired by George IV. This room is now used by the Knights of the Garter as their Robing Room before the procession to St George's Chapel on Garter Day.

PICTURES

Over door

1 After Sir Peter Lely, *Frances Stuart, Duchess of Richmond and Lennox,* c. 1678–80

Overmantel

2 After Pierre Mignard, *Elizabeth Charlotte, Princess Palatine, Duchess of Orleans, with her son, Philip and her daughter, Elizabeth,* c. 1660

Over door

3 Edmund Lilly, *William, Duke of Gloucester,* 1698

FURNITURE

4 Eight Venetian giltwood armchairs with embroidered velvet covers, early 18th century. Purchased by George IV in 1827

5 Pair of Boulle and lacquer cabinets, 18th and 19th centuries

THE QUEEN'S PRESENCE CHAMBER

Verrio's ceiling is his finest at Windsor and shows Catherine of Braganza seated in the centre. There are Grinling Gibbons carvings over the fireplace. The Gobelins tapestries are woven with Biblical scenes from the History of Esther.

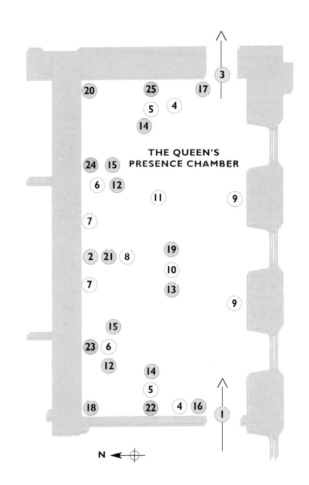

THE QUEEN'S PRESENCE CHAMBER

N ←⊕

6 Pair of English giltwood pier tables, c. 1760, purchased by Queen Mary from Chesterfield House in 1932, and probably originally from Stowe

7 Two English gilt gesso candle stands, early 18th century

8 Giltwood firescreen with Beauvais tapestry panel, late 18th century

9 Pair of English giltwood pier glasses, early 19th century

10 English rosewood and brass inlaid library table, c. 1820

11 Persian wool carpet, late 19th century

PORCELAIN

12 Pair of celadon porcelain candelabra with gilt bronze mounts by the Vulliamys, 1819

13 Chinese celadon porcelain dish, 14th century, with French gilt bronze mounts, c. 1730

14 Pair of celadon porcelain ewers with French gilt bronze mounts, 18th century

ABOVE: Bust of George Frideric Handel, by Louis François Roubiliac

15 Four Chinese celadon vases with French gilt bronze mounts, late 18th–early 19th century

SCULPTURE

16 White marble bust of G. F. Handel, by L. F. Roubiliac, 1739

17 White marble bust of John, Lord Ligonier, by L. F. Roubiliac, c. 1750

18 White marble bust of the duc de Villars, by A. Coysevox, 1718

19 Two French bronze groups of the Rape of the Sabines, after Giambologna, 18th century

20 White marble bust of Marshal Vauban, by A. Coysevox, 1706

21 White marble clock case designed by Robert Adam and carved by John Bacon the Elder, 1789. Originally in Queen Charlotte's Saloon at Buckingham House. Movement by B.Vulliamy

TAPESTRIES

Four Gobelins panels from the History of Esther, after J-F. de Troy, woven by Audran and Cozette, 1779–87

22 *The Banquet of Esther*

23 *The Disdain of Mordecai*

24 *The same panel repeated*

25 *The Judgement of Haman*

THE QUEEN'S GUARD CHAMBER

Originally there were two Guard Chambers, one at the entry to the King's apartments (on the site of the Grand Reception Room) and this, which was the entrance to the Queen's apartments. It was remodelled in the Gothic style with a plaster rib vault by Wyatville for George IV. Over the busts of Marlborough and Wellington hang replica French flags, the royal fleurs-de-lys for Marlborough and the tricolour for Wellington. These are presented each year to The Queen by the present Dukes as quit-rents for their estates at Blenheim and Stratfield Saye respectively. The chimneypiece is of polished Dent limestone. Wyatville added the large bay window over the State Entrance, which gives good views into the Quadrangle. Immediately opposite is the George IV Gateway, beyond which the axis is continued for three miles into the Great Park by the Long Walk. The display of arms on the walls derives from Sir Samuel Rush Meyrick's arrangement, which in turn was based on seventeenth-century ideas for the decorative use of arms in the Royal Armouries. The Indian ivory throne in the centre of the Guard Chamber was a present from the Maharajah of Travancore to Queen Victoria in 1851. Today the room is used for receptions of the Diplomatic Corps when they come to pay their respects to a visiting Head of State. The heralds change into their tabards here before the Garter Service in St George's Chapel.

BELOW: The Queen's Guard Chamber

THE QUEEN'S GUARD CHAMBER

The French flags over the busts of Marlborough and Wellington are presented each year by the present Dukes as 'rent' for their estates. The elaborate ivory throne was a present to Queen Victoria from the Maharajah of Travancore.

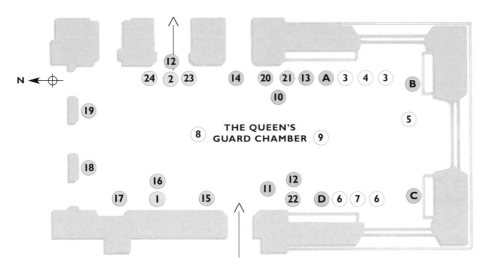

N ←⊕

THE QUEEN'S GUARD CHAMBER

PICTURES

1 Joachim Kayser and Johannes Anton von Klyher, *Frederick, Prince of Wales, on Horseback*, 1727 (overmantel)

2 Anon., Spanish School, 16th century, *Portrait of a Spanish Nobleman*

FURNITURE

3 Coronation thrones of Jacobean design made by Morris & Co. for King George V and Queen Mary and copied from a chair at Knole. Used in the second part of the Coronation, 22 June 1911

4 Throne with the arms of the Duke of Edinburgh. Made by Beresford & Hicks

5 Oak thrones of King George V, Queen Mary and Edward, Prince of Wales. Made by Morris & Co. for the Investiture of the Prince of Wales in 1911

6 Coronation thrones made by Howard & Sons for King George V and Queen Mary and copied from a chair at Knole. Used in the first part of the Coronation, 22 June 1911

7 The Waterloo Elm armchair. Made by Thomas Chippendale the Younger from part of the elm on the field of Waterloo. Presented to George IV in 1821

8 Gilt bronze chandelier by W. Perry, c. 1830

9 Indian ivory chair of state and footstool, presented to Queen Victoria in 1851 by the Maharajah of Travancore and shown at the Great Exhibition

ARMS & ARMOUR

10 Guidon of The Queen's Royal Irish Hussars

11 Colour of the Sovereign's Company of the Grenadier Guards

12 Trophies of firearms, armour and edged weapons, English, 18th–19th centuries

13 Range of display cabinets containing European armour, firearms and edged weapons. Mainly from the collection of George IV at Carlton House

A Case containing a 17th-century Italian child's half-armour, a display of 18th- and 19th-century small swords, and Henry VIII's hunting sword, made by Diego de Caias, 1544, and acquired by H. M. The Queen in 1966

B Case containing swords and daggers, including a dress sword with a mid-17th-century Dutch carved ivory hilt

C Case containing pistols, including several Scottish flintlock Highland pistols (Tacks), 1780 1800, and a pair of flintlock pistols by Diemar, c. 1780, with inlaid relief decoration to the stocks

D Case including a half-armour presented to Charles I when Prince of Wales by Charles Emanuel of Savoy

14 Japanese Samurai short sword, c. 1420. Surrendered by Field Marshal Count Terauchi to the Supreme Allied Commander, South-East Asia (Lord Louis Mountbatten) to mark the end of the War in the Far East, 1945

SCULPTURE

15 Bronze bust of Emperor Charles V by Leone Leoni, mid-16th century. Purchased by George IV in 1825

16 Patinated lead equestrian group of William Augustus, Duke of Cumberland, attributed to Henry Cheere, mid-18th century

17 Bronze bust of Philip II of Spain by Leone Leoni, mid-16th century. Purchased by George IV in 1825

18 Bronze bust of Ferdinand, Duke of Alba, by Leone Leoni, mid-16th century. Purchased by George IV in 1825

19 Bronze bust of Enea Caprara by Massimiliano Soldani-Benzi, c. 1695

20 White marble bust of Sir Winston Churchill, by Oscar Nemon, 1956. Commissioned by H.M. The Queen

21 White marble bust of John Churchill, 1st Duke of Marlborough, by John Henning, early 19th century. Beneath the annual rent banner for Blenheim Palace

22 White marble bust of Arthur, 1st Duke of Wellington, by Sir Francis Chantrey, 1835. Beneath the annual rent banner for Stratfield Saye House

METALWORK

23 Silver-plated replica of the Shield of Achilles, designed by John Flaxman, 19th century

24 German silver and enamel shield designed by P. von Cornelius, 1842. A christening present to King Edward VII from King Frederick William IV of Prussia

ABOVE: *Frederick, Prince of Wales, on Horseback*, by Joachim Kayser and Johannes Anton von Klyher, 1727

ST GEORGE'S HALL

St George's Hall is one of the most historic rooms in the Castle and has for six centuries been associated with the Order of the Garter. It occupies the site of Edward III's Great Hall and Chapel. These had been redecorated by Hugh May for Charles II, with murals by Verrio and carvings by Grinling Gibbons; they formed the climax of Baroque Windsor. The murals were very largely destroyed, except for a few areas which survived beneath the later plaster, when Wyatville knocked together the old Hall and Chapel in 1829 to create one enormously long room of over 55 metres (180 feet). One fragment of the ceiling, showing Charles II, has recently been reacquired by the Royal Collection. This romantic Gothic interior was inspired by Sir Walter Scott, whose novels, set in the Middle Ages, were greatly admired by George IV. When the interior of the Castle was remodelled in the 1820s by Wyatville, Gothic was chosen for all the processional spaces while eclectic classical was mainly used for the reception rooms. In St George's Hall, Wyatville's ceiling (of plaster grained to resemble oak) was decorated with the coats of arms of all the Knights of the Garter from their founda-

LEFT: St George's Hall after the restoration of 1997

ST GEORGE'S HALL

This occupies the site of Edward III's original Hall. The arms of all the Knights of the Garter decorate the ceiling. The roof is a new oak hammerbeam roof replacing Wyatville's, burnt in 1992. The Queen gives State Banquets in this room.

tion, a scheme devised by Thomas Willement, the King's heraldic artist. The walls were embellished with alternate trophies of weapons and figures in armour. An important addition to this scheme, as part of the recent restoration, is the equestrian figure of the King's Champion which now faces down the Hall from the new balcony at the east end. The Champion (an hereditary office held by the Dymoke family) used to ride into the Coronation Banquet in Westminster Hall, throw down his gauntlet three times and challenge anyone to deny the new sovereign. This ceremony last took place at George IV's Coronation in 1821.

St George's Hall was seriously damaged by the fire of 1992. The ceiling and the east wall, which contained a large double-sided organ by Father Willis, were destroyed. The new green oak roof has been designed by Giles Downes of the Sidell Gibson Partnership and is of hammerbeam construction. It is the largest oak hammerbeam roof to have been built in the twentieth century, and is more steeply pitched than Wyatville's. The overall

PICTURES

1 Sir Anthony Van Dyck, *James I*, c. 1635–6

2 Daniel Mytens, *Charles I*, 1631

3 Sir Peter Lely and a later hand, *Charles II*, c. 1672

4 Sir Peter Lely and Studio, *James II*, c. 1665–70

5 Sir Godfrey Kneller, *Mary II*, 1690

6 Sir Godfrey Kneller, *William III*, c. 1690

7 Studio of Sir Godfrey Kneller, *Queen Anne*, c. 1705

8 Studio of Sir Godfrey Kneller, *George I*, c. 1715

9 Enoch Seeman, *George II*, c. 1730

10 Gainsborough Dupont, *George III*, c. 1794

11 Sir Thomas Lawrence, *George IV*, c. 1825

SCULPTURE

Twenty-one marble busts of sovereigns and other royal members of the Order of the Garter

NORTH WALL

12 *Queen Anne*, attributed to J. M. Rysbrack, c. 1710

13 *George II*, by L. F. Roubiliac, c. 1750

14 *George III*, by John Bacon the Elder, 1775

15 *George IV*, by Francis Chantrey, 1826

16 *William IV*, by Francis Chantrey, 1837

17 *Queen Victoria*, by Edward Onslow Ford, 1898

18 *Albert, Prince Consort*, by R. W. Sevier, 1842

19 *Edward VII*, by Sidney March, 1902

20 *Alfred, Duke of Edinburgh*, by J. E. Boehm, 1879

21 *Leopold, Duke of Albany*, by F. J. Williamson, 1883

22 *Arthur, Duke of Connaught*, by F. J. Williamson, 1885

SOUTH WALL

23 *Frederick, Prince of Wales*, by Peter Scheemakers, c. 1733

24 *William, Duke of Cumberland*, by Joseph Nollekens, 1814 (copy of a bust by Rysbrack of 1754)

25 *Edward, Duke of York*, by Joseph Nollekens, 1766

26 *Frederick, Duke of York*, by J. C. Lochee, c. 1787

27 *Ernest, Duke of Cumberland*, by William Behnes, 1826

28 *Edward, Duke of Kent*, by William Behnes, 1828

29 *Augustus Frederick, Duke of Sussex*, by William Theed (posthumous), 1881

30 *Adolphus, Duke of Cambridge*, by Lawrence Macdonald, 1848

31 *George, Duke of Cambridge*, by G. G. Adams, 1888

32 *Frederick III, King of Prussia*, by W. White after R. Begas, 1897

FURNITURE

33 Massive carved oak chair of state known as 'Edward III's throne', c. 1835

ARMOUR

34 The armour of the King's Champion. Made at Greenwich in 1585 for Sir Christopher Hatton, and given by him to Robert Dudley, Earl of Leicester. It is supposed to have been used at the Coronation Banquets of George I and George II by members of the Dymoke family, Hereditary King's Champions. It was presented to Edward VII in 1901

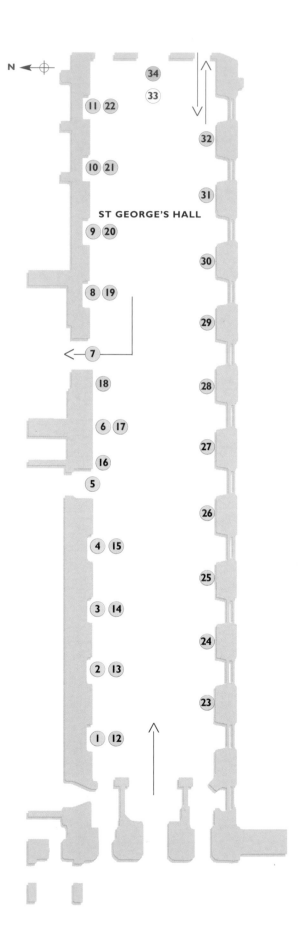

ST GEORGE'S HALL

ABOVE: Charles II, a fragment of Verrio's lost plaster ceiling in St George's Hall

proportions and appearance of the room are now considered greatly improved. The new oak screen at the east end, also designed by Giles Downes, supports oak carvings of the Queen's Beasts on the parapet; these were given by the City of London. The decorative plaster garter and rose in the gable was presented by the Commonwealth; each of the fifty-four petals represents a country. The new oak floor incorporates trees grown on the estates of Knights of the Garter. The scheme of shields of every Garter Knight has been re-created on the ceiling and is continued round the room. It is a vigorous example of heraldic decoration and is completed by the new heraldic stained glass created by John Reyntiens in the top lights of the windows. The side walls and west screen survived the fire and have been repaired. The full-length portraits and the marble busts form a royal pantheon, while Wyatville's great Gothic 'throne of Edward III' has been reinstated in its old position at the east end.

THE PRIVATE CHAPEL

Designed by Giles Downes of the Sidell Gibson Partnership as part of the restoration of the Castle following the 1992 fire, this is the private chapel of the Royal Family. Its intimate proportions give it something of the character of a little medieval chantry chapel. The altar apse neatly interlocks into the angle of the Lantern Lobby, and accommodates a new altar table by David Linley, while the stained glass window opposite, by Joseph Nuttgens, commemorates the fire of 1992 and subsequent restoration. The altarpiece is by Berto di Giovanni, a Perugian contemporary of Raphael, and was purchased by Queen Victoria in 1853. The Gothic chairs were designed for the Castle by the 15-year-old A. W. N. Pugin in 1827.

BELOW: The Private Chapel

THE PRIVATE CHAPEL

By virtue of its function as the Private Chapel of the Royal Family it is not possible to allow access to this room. The tour continues on p. 44.

THE LANTERN LOBBY

This new room, which occupies the site of Queen Victoria's Private Chapel, creates a new processional sequence through the Castle. The fire began here in November 1992, completely gutting the Chapel. Part of the carved stone reredos above the altar survived the flames and has been restored as a memorial to the conflagration. The inscription reads: 'The fire of 20th November 1992 began here. Restoration of the fire-damaged area was completed five years later, on 20th November 1997, the

RIGHT: The Lantern Lobby

fiftieth anniversary of the wedding of Her Majesty Queen Elizabeth II and His Royal Highness The Duke of Edinburgh.'

The new, tall, octagonal lobby created in the gutted area is inspired by Ely Cathedral and the Abbey of Batalha in Portugal. The result is a carefully proportioned space which neatly solves the problem of the change of axis in the north-east corner of the Castle between St George's Hall and the Royal Apartments to the south and east. Eight oak columns support a ribbed vault and a central glazed lantern. Though the feel is medieval, the finely executed and

LEFT: The inlaid marble centre to the floor

ARMOUR

1 Suit of armour made at Greenwich for Henry VIII, c. 1540

DISPLAY CASES

2 'Buffet' of silver gilt vessels and dishes, 17th–19th centuries, including a centrepiece designed by William Kent and made for Frederick, Prince of Wales, by George Wickes, 1745; a massive sideboard dish by William Pitts representing the Feast of the Gods; and a pair of Charles II firedogs adapted for George IV and engraved with his arms

3 Selection of standing cups, 16th–19th centuries, including a nautilus cup by Nicolaus Schmidt of Nuremberg; a 17th-century German carved ivory cup from William Beckford's collection at Fonthill Abbey; the National Cup, designed by John Flaxman, 1824;

and the Dürer Cup, designed by A. W. N. Pugin (based on a design by Albrecht Dürer), 1826–7 (the last two supplied by Rundell, Bridge & Rundell)

4 Selection from the Private Chapel Plate of Windsor Castle, Buckingham Palace and Brighton Pavilion, English, 17th–19th centuries

5 Selection of English and French silver gilt toilet wares, including a travelling toilet service that belonged to Queen Mary II, c. 1690 and later, and items with Napoleonic associations

PICTURES

6 George Weymouth, *Prince Philip, Duke of Edinburgh*, 1995

SCULPTURE

7 Bronze bust of Her Majesty The Queen by John Dowie of Adelaide, 1987

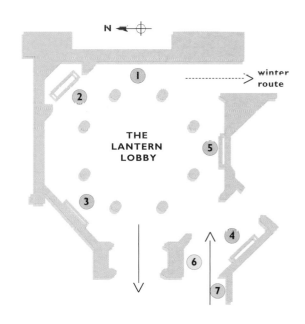

THE LANTERN LOBBY
This modern Gothic room replaces the Private Chapel gutted by fire in 1992. Part of the Victorian reredos survives as a memorial. It was inspired by the Octagon at Ely and the new rib vault is of laminated oak. The display of silver gilt plate includes special commissions of George IV.

ABOVE: The Lantern

ABOVE: The reredos of the former chapel, incorporating the inscribed tablet

original detail celebrates modern Gothic design and British crafts-manship, especially in the joinery of the columns and vault, and in such features as the stamped red leather and delicate ironwork of the central doors to St George's Hall. There is also a finely inlaid floor of English marbles depicting the Garter Star, but this is sometimes overlaid with an octagonal carpet of similar pattern, made at Axmin-ster for the new room in 1997.

The Lobby has been partly conceived as a treasury with wall cases to display silver gilt from the Royal Collection, including chapel and buffet plate and some of George IV's more unusual commissions such as Flaxman's National Cup (1824). On axis with the central door from St George's Hall stands Henry VIII's armour, a masterpiece from the workshop established by the King at Greenwich.

THE NEW CORRIDOR

Here hang four portraits, two by Ramsay and one each by Reynolds and Zoffany: attributed to Allan Ramsay, *Elizabeth Albertina, Princess of Mecklenberg-Strelitz, c. 1760*; Johann Zoffany, *Prince Ernest of Mecklenberg-Strelitz, c. 1772*; Sir Joshua Reynolds, *George III, c. 1780*; Allan Ramsay, *Prince George Augustus of Mecklenberg-Strelitz, c. 1769*.

THE SEMI-STATE ROOMS

These were created by George IV in the 1820s as part of a new series of Royal Apartments for his personal occupation. Designed by Wyatville, they were dec-orated and furnished by Morel and Seddon. They continue in use by The Queen for official entertaining. Damaged in the 1992 fire, they have been restored to their original appearance and contain furniture and works of art chosen by George IV.

These rooms are open only in the winter months. At other times, the tour continues on p.54.

THE GREEN DRAWING ROOM

(Viewed from the Crimson Drawing Room, through the doors to the right.)

ABOVE: Sèvres Louis XVI service. Detail showing mirror, Desjardins candelabra and cabinet with porcelain

THE GREEN DRAWING ROOM

This room is used by The Queen for official entertaining, and is one of a series of superbly decorated and furnished rooms created for George IV. The Axminster carpet was shown at the Great Exhibition in 1851.

This room largely survived the fire but was saturated by water. The opportunity has been taken to replace the silk for the walls and redesign the window curtains to match more closely the Morel and Seddon scheme designed for George IV, who intended this room as a library. After the establishment of the new Royal Library, the book-cases were adapted to display another of his acquisitions, the Sèvres service made for Louis XVI, which is one of the finest in existence.

The gilded ceiling by Wyatville is his most accomplished at Windsor. There is a tautness and perfection of detail in the work executed during George IV's lifetime that is lacking from the state rooms decorated in the next reign. The seat furniture is part of a huge set commissioned by George IV from Morel and Seddon. The bronzes were mainly assembled by George IV and include the Four Seasons by Desjardins mounted as candelabra by Caffieri for the comte d'Orsay. The Axminster carpet was designed by Ludwig Gruner for Queen Victoria and shown at the Great Exhibition in 1851, where it was greatly admired as an excellent example of English manufacture. It survived the fire of 1992 but is now too delicate to allow visitors to walk on it.

ABOVE: *The Family of Queen Victoria in 1887*, by Laurits Regner Tuxen

BELOW: The Green Drawing Room

THE CRIMSON DRAWING ROOM

This was the principal room in George IV's semi-state rooms. The general form of the room – a long rectangle with a broad bay window overlooking the East Terrace Garden – was designed by Jeffry Wyatville, but the decoration was entrusted to Morel and Seddon. They were responsible for the wall decorations, including the framed panels of silk, and the window curtains. The room also incorporates fittings from Carlton House, notably the black marble and bronze chimneypiece by the Vulliamys (a pair to that in the Green Drawing Room) and the four pairs of carved and gilded doors. This room, like the Green Drawing Room, is very much an expression of George IV's personal taste, reflecting the spirit of some of the drawing rooms at Carlton House. It was severely damaged in the 1992 fire. The ceiling collapsed and large areas of the walls were badly calcined. The restoration has been carried out by Donald Insall and Partners, a firm of specialist conservation architects which has been responsible for all the restoration, as opposed to the new work, in the fire-damaged part of the Castle. The opportunity has been taken to reweave the silk damask wall hangings to the striped pattern and rich crimson colour chosen for the room by George IV. Window curtains of the same material have also been reinstated to designs which reflect the lavishness of Morel and Seddon's original scheme, using photographs of the room taken in 1867. The new curtains and rich *passementerie* were devised by Pamela Lewis, who has been responsible for the design of all the upholstery restoration. The reinstated ceiling incorporates many fragments of the original plasterwork by Bernasconi, salvaged from the debris after the fire.

As intended by George IV, the room is furnished with Morel and Seddon's seat furniture, and also sumptuous French

BELOW: State portraits of Queen Elizabeth and George VI, by Sir Gerald Kelly, 1942–5

ABOVE: *Princess Elizabeth*, by Sir William Beechey, 1795–7

works of art including three pairs of *pietra dura* and ebony cabinets and six ormolu candelabra by Thomire. The vast crystal chandelier, though made for George IV, was hung here earlier this century by Queen Mary. It was severely damaged in the fire but has now been completely restored. The overall *mise-en-scène* evokes the splendour of Carlton House to a remarkable degree. This and the adjoining rooms are the finest and most complete examples in existence of late-Georgian taste in decoration, and the recent restoration has enhanced their quality as a sequence of inter-related spaces.

PICTURES

1 Sir William Beechey, *Princess Augusta*, 1795–7

2 Sir William Beechey, *Princess Mary*, 1795–7

3 Sir Gerald Kelly, *George VI*, 1942–5

4 Sir William Beechey, *Princess Sophia*, 1795–7

5 Sir William Beechey, *Princess Amelia*, 1795–7

6 Sir Gerald Kelly, *Queen Elizabeth, Queen Consort of King George VI*, 1942–5

7 Sir William Beechey, *Princess Elizabeth*, 1795–7

8 Sir William Beechey, *Charlotte, Princess Royal, c.* 1795–7

9 John Hoppner, *Edward, Duke of Kent, c.* 1800

10 After John Hoppner, *George IV when Prince of Wales, c.* 1800

THE CRIMSON DRAWING ROOM

This is The Queen's principal drawing room at Windsor. From the bay window there is a good view over the private East Terrace Garden. The furniture was acquired by George IV. The marble fireplace and carved and gilt doors come from his London residence at Carlton House.

CHIMNEYPIECE

Polished black marble, patinated and gilt bronze, with figures of satyrs to either side. Supplied by the Vulliamys in 1807–12 for the Crimson Drawing Room at Carlton House

FURNITURE

Pieces from a set of upholstered, carved and gilt beechwood seat furniture by Morel & Seddon, *c.* 1829

11 Two rectangular sofa tables with inlaid amboyna tops and gilt bronze mounts, by Morel & Seddon, *c.* 1829

12 Two circular tables with gilt bronze mounts, by Morel & Seddon, *c.* 1829

13 Six tall French Empire gilt bronze candelabra (two of eleven lights; four of fourteen) of antique form, by Pierre-Philippe Thomire. From the Throne Room and Old Throne Room at Carlton House. Purchased by George IV in 1814

14 Pair of French Empire seven-light lapis lazuli and gilt bronze candelabra

by Pierre-Philippe Thomire. Purchased by George IV in 1817

15 French Empire gilt bronze clock representing the Spirit of the Arts and inscribed *Artium Genio*, by Pierre-Philippe Thomire. Bought by George IV in 1813. From the Throne Room at Carlton House

16 Pair of French ebony cabinets with gilt bronze mounts and *pietra dura* panels, 1803. Acquired from M-E. Lignereux for George IV by Sir Harry Featherstonhaugh

17 Pair of English ebony and *pietra dura* cabinets attributed to Robert Hume, *c.* 1820. Purchased for George IV in 1825

18 Smaller pair of ebony, Boulle and *pietra dura* cabinets attributed to Robert Hume, *c.* 1820

19 An English carved and gilt beechwood pedestal supported by three winged griffins, attributed to Tatham, Bailey & Sanders, *c.* 1811

20 Large cut-glass and gilt bronze 28-light chandelier, *c.* 1810

PORCELAIN

21 Large Chinese dark blue porcelain vase mounted as a tripod. The gilt bronze mounts are attributed to P-P. Thomire, *c.* 1790

22 Pair of tall late-18th-century Sèvres porcelain vases with gilt bronze mounts

23 Pair of tall dark blue Sèvres porcelain covered vases (*vase bachelier*), *c.* 1767–70

SCULPTURE

24 Bronze figure of *Mars* attributed to Sebastien Slodtz, early 18th century

25 Bronze figure of Julius Caesar by Nicolas Couston, early 18th century

THE CRIMSON DRAWING ROOM

THE STATE DINING ROOM

In contrast to the drawing rooms, George IV chose the Gothic style for this room. The juxtaposition of Gothic and classical decoration was an aspect of George IV's taste also to be found at Carlton House. The room was gutted in the 1992 fire, as it had been (though less badly) on a previous occasion in 1853. The largest of the sideboards, being too big to move, was destroyed, as was Beechey's painting hanging above, *George III at a Review*. The sideboard has been remade by the firm of N. E. J. Stevenson.

The room has been restored to Wyatville's design with its cambered, cusped and coffered ceiling, all painted stone colour and gold. The opportunity has been taken to restore important original details removed earlier this century in an attempt to lighten the room. These included the pilaster strips on the walls vigorously modelled with gilded vines and grapes. The crimson

BELOW: *The Family of Frederick, Prince of Wales,* by George Knapton, 1751

ABOVE: Benjamin Constant's portrait of Queen Victoria over the chimneypiece

curtains and crimson Gothic carpet reflect the original Morel and Seddon scheme, again using photographs taken in 1867. The sideboards and side tables were all designed in 1827 for Morel and Seddon by the young A. W. N. Pugin, whose first work this was. He later disowned this juvenilia, though admitting that 'the parts were correct and exceedingly well executed'. They comprise the best Gothic revival furniture of their date in Europe. Since the fire, the large St Petersburg porcelain vase has been placed in the north window. It shows Russian palaces and was a gift from Tsar Nicholas I to Queen Victoria. The bronze lamps round the room were made in 1810 by the Vulliamys for George IV at Carlton House. The huge group portrait over the sideboard is *The Family of Frederick, Prince of Wales*, by George Knapton.

PICTURES

1   George Knapton, *The Family of Frederick, Prince of Wales*, 1751. The recently widowed Augusta, Princess of Wales, poses with her children in front of a portrait of the deceased Prince Frederick which also depicts their home, the White House at Kew. The future King George III is second from the left

2   Benjamin Constant, *Queen Victoria*, 1899

FURNITURE

Suite of Gothic revival rosewood and partly gilt dining-room furniture (dining table, sideboards, wine coolers and serving tables) with gilt bronze mounts by Morel & Seddon from designs by the young A. W. N. Pugin, c. 1827. The very large sideboard beneath the Knapton portrait is a modern replica by N. E. J. Stevenson of the original, which was destroyed in the 1992 fire

3   Gilt beechwood dining chairs originally supplied for Carlton House by Tatham & Bailey, 1815

4   Eight patinated bronze lamps by the Vulliamys, 1810, on modern scagliola pedestals

5   French mantel clock with Sèvres porcelain panels depicting the history of timekeeping (*Pendule de L'Horlogerie*), presented to Queen Victoria by King Louis-Philippe at Windsor Castle in 1844

6   Pair of patinated bronze candelabra with figures of the Infant Hercules and the serpent, by the Vulliamys, c. 1810

PORCELAIN

7   Massive Russian porcelain vase with gilt bronze handles and mounts, painted with views of Peterhof and Tsarskoe Selo. Presented to Queen Victoria by Tsar Nicholas I in 1844

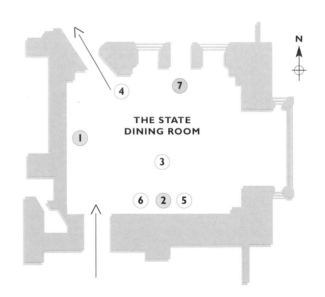

THE STATE DINING ROOM

Like the drawing rooms, this is used by The Queen for official entertaining. Wyatville's Gothic design has been restored following the 1992 fire which gutted the room. The sideboards were designed by the 15-year-old A. W. N. Pugin.

THE OCTAGON DINING ROOM

The Brunswick Tower, in which this room is situated, was an addition by Wyatville. There was no medieval precedent for an octagonal tower here. It is the most satisfying of Wyatville's smaller Gothic rooms. It too was gutted in 1992, when the Brunswick Tower became a huge chimney for the smoke and flames in the last and most dramatic episode of the fire. All the floors collapsed and the flames shot 15 metres (50 feet) into the sky above the battlements. Despite the severity of the blaze, Wyatville's dark marble Gothic chimneypiece and the stone tracery of the windows survived. Fortunately the original furnishings were in store. The room has therefore been reinstated according to Wyatville's plans. The Gothic oak furniture was designed by the young Pugin in 1827 and made by Morel and Seddon. The magnificent gilt metal Gothic chandelier, also by Pugin, was buried under 3 metres (10 feet) of rubble in the Private Chapel. It has now been restored and replaced here in the room for which it was made.

ABOVE: The Octagon Dining Room

THE OCTAGON DINING ROOM

N

FURNITURE

1 Set of Gothic revival stools, made of oak and pollard oak by Morel & Seddon, c. 1827, from designs by the young A. W. N. Pugin

2 Three Gothic revival oak side tables, veneered in pollard oak, by Morel & Seddon, c. 1827

3 Set of Gothic revival oak chairs with arcaded backs, mid-19th century

4 Oak extending dining table by Johnstone Norman & Co., 1891

CLOCK

5 Gilt bronze, white marble and Derby biscuit porcelain mantel clock by Benjamin Vulliamy, c. 1789

CHANDELIER

6 Gilt bronze Gothic revival chandelier designed by A. W. N. Pugin, and made by Hancock & Rixon, c. 1827

THE CHINA CORRIDOR

This narrow passage was added by Wyatville, outside the medieval curtain wall. The Gothic cases formerly housed George IV's armour collection, now in the Grand Vestibule and Queen's Guard Chamber; Queen Mary adapted them for the display of porcelain. This area survived the fire, suffering only limited damage.

THE GRAND RECEPTION ROOM

BELOW: The Grand
Reception Room

T his room, perhaps more than any other of the state rooms at Windsor, represents George IV's personal, francophile taste. It was designed under the King's immediate supervision with the assistance of Sir Charles Long, who bought eighteenth-century French panelling in Paris in 1825 specially for the wall decorations. This was incorporated with composition stucco by Francis Bernasconi to match, making a complete frame-

BELOW: The Grand
Reception Room

work for six Gobelins tapestries from the Jason series which were also bought in Paris by Long. Bernasconi modelled the elaborate plaster cove and ceiling, which were severely damaged in the 1992 fire but have been painstakingly restored. The gilded ornaments were designed by Frederick and John Crace, who previously worked for George IV at Brighton Pavilion.

Wyatville himself was rather ambivalent about all this gilded splendour. His assistant Henry Ashton later remarked: 'the introduction of French boiserie … would never have appeared in the castle had the architect been solely guided by his own judgement'. This impressive 'Louis Quatorze' decoration was, however, a great

TAPESTRIES

Six episodes from the Story of Jason, woven at the Gobelins factory in Paris between 1776 and 1779, by Cozette and Audran, after paintings by Jean-François de Troy. Purchased in Paris for George IV in 1825 (*The numbers in brackets place the episodes in the order of the legend*)

1 Jason, unfaithful to Medea, marries Glauce, daughter of King Creon of Thebes (4)

2 Soldiers sprung from the dragon's tooth turn their weapons against each other (2)

3 Medea stabs her two sons by Jason, sets fire to Corinth and departs for Athens (6)

4 Jason pledges his faith to Medea, who promises to help him with her sorcery (1)

5 Glauce is brought to death by the magic robe presented to her by Medea (5)

6 Jason puts the dragon to sleep, takes possession of the Golden Fleece and departs with Medea (3)

FURNITURE

7 Pair of giltwood tables with marble tops and griffin supports by Tatham, Bailey & Sanders, 1814. Made for Carlton House.

8 Pair of giltwood tables with marble tops and sphinx supports, mid-18th century and later

9 Two large circular tables by Morel & Seddon, with inlaid amboyna tops and winged lion supports, c. 1828

10 Chinoiserie gilt bronze clock and matching thermometer with painted bronze figures of a peacock and a Chinese man and a lady. Supplied by Vulliamy for Brighton Pavilion, 1830

11 Three massive English gilt bronze and cut-glass chandeliers, c. 1830

12 Pieces from two suites of upholstered giltwood seat furniture (some with gilt metal enrichments) by Morel & Seddon, 1829, covered with late 18th-century Beauvais tapestry. The set was extended for George V and Queen Mary in the 1920s

13 Aubusson flat-woven floral carpet with the cypher of King George V

14 Two pairs of late 18th-century Chinese dark blue porcelain vases, mounted as candelabra; the gilt bronze chinoiserie mounts by the Vulliamys, 1819. From Brighton Pavilion

15 Pair of Chinese blue porcelain candelabra with 18th-century French gilt bronze mounts

16 Pair of 18th-century Sèvres porcelain candelabra with gilt bronze mounts

17 Garnitures of late 18th-century French marble vases with gilt bronze mounts

SCULPTURE

18 Massive Russian urn veneered with malachite, presented to Queen Victoria by Tsar Nicholas I in 1839

19 Bronze group of Louis XV supported on a shield, by Jean-Baptiste Lemoyne, 1776

20 Bronze bust of the Prince de Conde, after Jerome Derbais, early 18th century (brought with no. 21 from Carlton House in 1828)

21 Bronze bust of Marshal Turenne after Jerome Derbais, early 18th century

22 Bronze bust of Cardinal Richelieu attributed to Jean Varin, 17th century

23 Bronze bust of Charles I after Hubert Le Sueur, ? 17th century

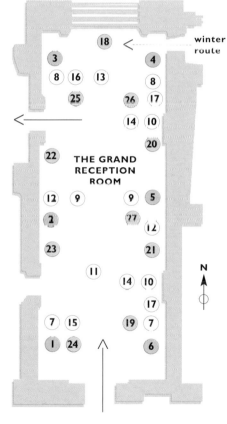

24 Bronze group of *The Abduction of Persephone by Pluto*, French, 18th century

25 Bronze group of *Hercules, Antaeus and Gaea*, French, 18th century

26 Bronze group of *Pluto and Persephone* after Girardon, French, 18th century

27 Pair of bronze vases in the form of grotesque figures, French, 18th century

THE GRAND RECEPTION ROOM

The Queen greets her guests in this room before a State Banquet. The French-style decoration was George IV's personal choice. The ceiling collapsed in the 1992 fire but has been accurately restored. The huge green malachite vase was a present from Tsar Nicholas I.

success, starting a fashion in London and English country houses that lasted throughout the nineteenth century.

As part of the post-1992 restoration all the gilding has been renewed and the room can now be seen in George IV's original dazzling splendour. The three superb gilt bronze and glass chandeliers collapsed in the fire but have been meticulously pieced together. The parquetry floor round the edge of the room is the original; blocks singed in the fire have been reversed. The huge malachite urn in the window is one of the largest outside Russia and was given to Queen Victoria by Tsar Nicholas I. It was too heavy to move, but survived with only superficial damage.

The room was intended by George IV as a ballroom and is now used by The Queen to greet her guests before State Banquets.

ABOVE: Gobelins tapestry: *Jason pledges his faith to Medea*

BELOW: Giltwood table with griffin supports, by Tatham, Bailey & Sanders, 1814

THE GARTER THRONE ROOM

ABOVE: State portrait of Her Majesty The Queen by Sir James Gunn, 1954–6

RIGHT: The Garter Throne Room

This was formed by Wyatville out of the first two of Charles II's state rooms, the King's Presence Chamber and the King's Privy or Audience Chamber; the shallow arch in front of the throne marks the line of the old wall between the two rooms. Wyatville removed Verrio's rich painted ceilings, which were deemed in bad condition, and replaced them with moulded plaster ceilings of his own design, ingeniously making use of the insignia and collar of the Order of the Garter (as he had already done in the ceiling of the drawing room at Badminton in 1811). Grinling Gibbons' seventeenth-century carved cornice survives or was copied, as does the wainscot of the dado, but the principal oak wall panels (together with the gilt wall lights and chandeliers) were inserted by Queen Mary to replace blue damask panels. The fine wood carvings are all reused from elsewhere; examples are the festoons over the fireplace surrounding a state portrait of The Queen and the more delicate panels incorporating the Garter Star over the doors flanking the throne. When George IV acceded to the

THE GARTER THRONE ROOM
In this room new Knights and Ladies of the Garter are invested with the insignia of the Order by The Queen. The room was re-modelled by Wyatville for William IV.

ABOVE: *Queen Victoria Investing Louis-Philippe with the Garter, 11 October 1844*, by Louis Haghe

throne and embarked on the reconstruction of Buckingham Palace and Windsor Castle, he sent many fixtures and fittings from his former London residence, Carlton House, to Windsor for incorporation in the new rooms there. The carved and gilt throne canopy was made originally for King George III's Audience Chamber at Windsor. It is in this room that The Queen invests new Knights and Ladies of the Garter with the insignia of the Order, before their installation in St George's Chapel on Garter Day.

ABOVE: *Model of the Arch of Constantine, 1815*, by Giovacchino and Pietro Belli

PICTURES

1   Gainsborough Dupont, *George III*, 1795

2   Studio of Sir Thomas Lawrence, *George IV*, c. 1818

3   Sir Martin Archer Shee, *William IV*, 1833

4   Sir James Gunn, *Queen Elizabeth II*, 1954–6

5   Franz Xaver Winterhalter, *Prince Albert*, 1843

6   Franz Xaver Winterhalter, *Queen Victoria*, 1843

7   Studio of Sir Godfrey Kneller, *George I*, c. 1715

8   Sir Godfrey Kneller, *George II*, 1716

FURNITURE

9   Giltwood armchairs by Charles Elliott, 1807

10 Three giltwood pier tables, early 19th century

11 Giltwood stools, late 18th century

12 Giltwood throne canopy, late 18th century, with 19th-century velvet hangings

13 Giltwood throne chair, made by White, Allom & Co. for the Coronation of Queen Elizabeth II, 1953

14 Three giltwood chandeliers, copied from an 18th-century original at Hampton Court, 20th century

SCULPTURE

Three white marble and gilt bronze models of Roman triumphal arches by G. and P. Belli, 1808–15. Acquired by George IV in 1815. Formerly in the Library at Carlton House

15 The Arch of Constantine

16 The Arch of Titus

17 The Arch of Septimius Severus

PORCELAIN

18 Pair of Chinese powder blue porcelain vases with French gilt bronze mounts, mid-18th century. Purchased by Queen Mary in 1920

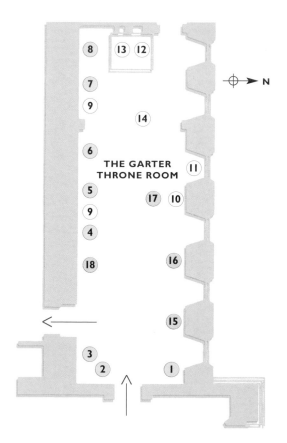

THE GARTER THRONE ROOM

THE WATERLOO CHAMBER

his room, dominated by the portrait of the 1st Duke of Wellington, was conceived by George IV to commemorate the defeat of Napoleon. He commissioned portraits from Sir Thomas Lawrence of the Allied monarchs, statesmen and commanders who had contributed to the victory. Lawrence travelled round Europe to create this bravura series of more than twenty portraits; Pius VII is considered to be his masterpiece.

It was part of Sir Charles Long's brief for the reconstruction of the Castle that a setting be created for Lawrence's portraits, and for an annual banquet on the anniversary of Waterloo on 18 June. Wyatville chose the larger of Edward III's inner courtyards – Horn Court – and roofed it over with an ingenious timber ceiling containing a raking clerestory reminiscent of ship's carpentry.

BELOW: The Waterloo Chamber prepared for a Garter Day Lunch

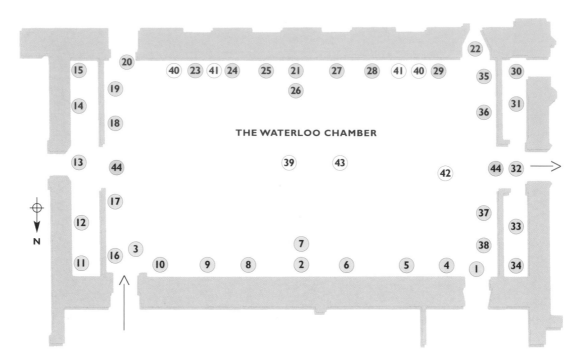

THE WATERLOO CHAMBER

PICTURES

NORTH WALL UPPER ROW

1 Sir Thomas Lawrence, *Louis-Antoine, Duke of Angoulême*, 1825

2 William Corden, *Frederick William, Duke of Brunswick*, 1848

3 Sir Thomas Lawrence, *Prince Leopold of Saxe-Coburg, later King of the Belgians*, 1821

NORTH WALL LOWER ROW

4 Sir Thomas Lawrence, *Adolphus, Duke of Cambridge*, 1818

5 Sir Thomas Lawrence, *Robert Banks Jenkinson, 2nd Earl of Liverpool, c.* 1820

6 Sir David Wilkie, *William IV*, 1832

7 Sir Thomas Lawrence, *George III, c.* 1820

8 Studio of Sir Thomas Lawrence, *George IV, c.* 1820

9 Sir Thomas Lawrence, *Robert Stewart, Viscount Castlereagh, c.* 1817

10 Sir Thomas Lawrence, *Frederick, Duke of York*, 1816

EAST WALL UPPER ROW

11 Robert McInnes, *General Sir James Kempt*, 1836

12 Sir Thomas Lawrence, *Matvei Ivanovitch, Count Platov*, 1814

13 Sir Thomas Lawrence, *Arthur Wellesley, 1st Duke of Wellington*, 1814–15

14 Sir Thomas Lawrence, *Field Marshal Gebhardt von Blücher*, 1814

15 James Lonsdale, *Sir William Congreve, c.* 1805–10

EAST WALL LOWER ROW

16 Sir Thomas Lawrence, *Charles William, Baron von Humboldt*, 1828

17 After Sir Thomas Lawrence, *George Canning, c.* 1830

18 Sir Thomas Lawrence, *Henry, 3rd Earl Bathurst, c.* 1820

19 Sir Thomas Lawrence, *Ernest Frederick, Count Münster*, 1820

SOUTH WALL UPPER ROW

20 Sir Martin Archer Shee, *Henry Paget, 2nd Earl of Uxbridge and 1st Marquess of Anglesey*, 1836

21 Sir Thomas Lawrence, *Alexander Ivanovitch, Prince Chernichev*, 1818

22 Nicaise de Keyser, *William II, King of the Netherlands, when Prince of Orange*, 1846

SOUTH WALL LOWER ROW

23 Sir Thomas Lawrence, *Ercole, Cardinal Consalvi*, 1819

24 Sir Thomas Lawrence, *Charles Augustus, Prince Hardenberg*, 1818

25 Sir Thomas Lawrence, *The Emperor Alexander I of Russia*, 1814–18

26 Sir Thomas Lawrence, *The Emperor Francis I of Austria*, 1818–19

27 Sir Thomas Lawrence, *Frederick William III of Prussia*, 1814–18

28 Sir Thomas Lawrence, *Charles Robert, Count Nesselrode*, 1818

29 Sir Thomas Lawrence, *Pope Pius VII*, 1819

WEST WALL UPPER ROW

30 Henry William Pickersgill, *General Viscount Hill, c.* 1830

31 Sir Thomas Lawrence, *Charles X of France*, 1825

32 Sir Thomas Lawrence, *Charles Philip, Prince Schwarzenberg*, 1819

33 Sir Thomas Lawrence, *Charles, Archduke of Austria*, 1819

34 Sir Martin Archer Shee, *Sir Thomas Picton*, 1836

WEST WALL LOWER ROW

35 Sir Thomas Lawrence, *John, Count Capo D'Istria*, 1818–19

36 Sir Thomas Lawrence, *Clemens Lothar Wenzel, Prince Metternich*, 1819

37 Sir Thomas Lawrence, *Armand Emmanuel, Duke of Richelieu*, 1818

38 Sir Thomas Lawrence, *General Theodore Petrovitch Uvarov*, 1818

FURNITURE

39 Mahogany extending dining table by Thomas Dowbiggin, 1846

40 Giltwood sofas and armchairs in the style of A. W. N. Pugin, *c.* 1830

41 Two giltwood side tables with marble tops, 18th and 19th centuries

42 Indian (Agra) carpet, presented to Queen Victoria, 1894

43 Set of six French gilt bronze tripod tazzas, early 19th century

SCULPTURE

44 Limewood panels and drops, some by Grinling Gibbons and workshop

ABOVE: The Princesses
Elizabeth (now Queen
Elizabeth II) and Margaret
with Queen Elizabeth
during a wartime
pantomime rehearsal in
the Waterloo Chamber,
December 1941

The panelling round the lower part of the room incorporates seventeenth-century wood carvings by Grinling Gibbons and his workshop salvaged from Charles II's demolished Chapel, such as the palm fronds over the large doors at either end. The 'Elizabethan' fretted plaster decoration on the upper walls and the unusual glass chandeliers, by Osler, were added by Queen Victoria.

The room is used for the annual luncheon for the Knights of the Garter and their spouses in June, when the table — decorated with silver gilt, flowers, and china from one of the historic services in the Royal Collection — is set for fifty to sixty guests. The room is also used for concerts and balls. This and all the rooms at Windsor look their best *en fête* for the great occasions for which they were intended.

BELOW: *Arthur Wellesley,
1st Duke of Wellington,* by
Sir Thomas Lawrence,
1814–15

THE WATERLOO CHAMBER

This, the largest room at Windsor, celebrates the victory of the Allies in 1815. The portraits by Sir Thomas Lawrence include the Duke of Wellington and the other commanders, monarchs and statesmen who contributed to Napoleon's defeat. The Queen holds an annual luncheon here for the Garter Knights and Ladies.

ENGINE COURT AND THE QUADRANGLE

After leaving the State Apartments, the Quadrangle can be seen from the low iron railings across the north-west corner. Diagonally opposite is the Sovereign's Entrance, which gives access to the private Royal Apartments on the south and east sides. All along the south and east sides is the Grand Corridor added by Wyatville for George IV to improve the communications between the different parts of the Castle. The bronze equestrian statue of Charles II was cast in 1679 by Josiah Ibach, a German. It surveys the Quadrangle from the foot of the motte. Wyatville's granite plinth incorporates a small fountain and carved marble panels by Grinling Gibbons. The Quadrangle provides the setting for many colourful ceremonies. When a foreign Head of State pays a State Visit he or she takes the salute here at a rank past of the Royal Horse Artillery, followed by the Sovereign's Escort of the Household Cavalry and a march past of the Guard of Honour. When The Queen is in official residence the Changing of the Guard takes place in the Quadrangle. The Guard is frequently formed from a battalion of one of the Household regiments.

BELOW: The Quadrangle

ST GEORGE'S CHAPEL

St George's Chapel is the spiritual home of the Order of the Garter, Britain's senior Order of Chivalry, founded by King Edward III in 1348. St George is the patron saint of the Order.

The building of the Chapel was begun by King Edward IV in 1475. By 1484 the Choir was finished, roofed in wood. His son-in-law, King Henry VII, completed the nave and added the stone-vaulted ceiling throughout before his death in 1509. King Henry VIII completed the building by 1528.

The architecture of the Chapel ranks among the finest examples of Perpendicular Gothic, the late medieval style of English architecture.

As Sovereign of the Order of the Garter, The Queen attends a service here in June each year, together with the Knights and Ladies of the Order. Ten sovereigns are buried in the Chapel, all represented by magnificent tombs.

A separate guide-book is available.

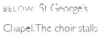

BELOW: St George's Chapel. The choir stalls

THE ALBERT MEMORIAL CHAPEL

The richly decorated interior of this fifteenth-century chapel was created by George Gilbert Scott for Queen Victoria to commemorate her husband Prince Albert, who died in 1861. The vaulted ceiling has gold mosaic by Antonio Salviati. The inlaid marble panels by Henri de Triqueti around the lower walls depict scenes from Scripture. The marble effigy of Prince Albert himself is also by Triqueti.

The Chapel is now dominated by Alfred Gilbert's masterpiece, the tomb of the Duke of Clarence and Avondale (elder son of Edward VII).

THE LOWER WARD

The Lower Ward is occupied by the College of St George, founded by Edward III as part of the Order of the Garter. On the left, as one descends the hill, are the lodgings of the Military Knights, and beyond is the Henry

ABOVE: The Albert Memorial Chapel

VIII Gateway. At the bottom is the Guard House (1862). Most of the right-hand side is occupied by St George's Chapel and the Albert Memorial Chapel. Behind is a warren of medieval cloisters and buildings forming the houses and offices of the clergy attached to the Chapel, including the choir school. These have developed over the centuries out of Henry III's buildings in the Lower Ward.

BELOW: The annual procession of the Knights of the Garter